Ultimate SLOWCOOKER

Ultimate SLOWCOOKER

Over 100 simple, delicious recipes

Sara Lewis

hamlyn

An Hachette UK Company
www.hachette.co.uk

First published in Great Britain in 2008 by
Hamlyn, a division of Octopus Publishing Group Ltd,
Endeavour House, 189 Shaftesbury Avenue,
London WC2H 8JY
www.octopusbooks.co.uk
Copyright © 2008 Octopus Publishing Limited

ISBN: 978-0-600-61895-9

A CIP catalogue record for this book is available
from the British Library

Printed in China

10 9 8 7 6 5

This material was previously published as *Slow Cooker* and *Slow Cooker Easy*.

Notes

Standard level spoon measures are used in all the recipes
1 tablespoon = one 15 ml spoon
1 teaspoon = one 5 ml spoon

Both metric and imperial measurements are given for the recipes. Use one set
of measures only, not a mixture of both.

A few recipes include nuts and nut derivatives. Anyone with a known nut allergy
must avoid these. It is advisable for people with known allergic reactions to
nuts and nut derivatives and those who may be particularly vulnerable to avoid
dishes made with nuts and nut oils. It is also prudent to check the labels of
pre-prepared ingredients for the possible inclusion of nut derivatives.

Read your slow cooker manual before you begin and preheat the slow cooker
if required according to the manufacturer's instructions. Because slow cookers
vary slightly from manufacturer to manufacturer, check recipe timings with the
manufacturer's directions for a recipe using the same main ingredient.

All the recipes for this book were tested in slow cookers with a working
capacity of 2.5 litres (4 pints), total capacity of 3.5 litres (6 pints).

Contents

Introduction

We all want to eat healthily, but at times this can seem impossible. The pressures of running a home and, probably, holding down a job, can make spending time in the kitchen the last thing we want to do when we get home. A call to return to home cooking and leave the nutritionally low, chilled ready meals on the supermarket shelves may seem to be flying in the face of experience. But home cooking needn't mean spending hours slaving away in the kitchen. Just 15–20 minutes are all that are needed to prepare a tasty meal that can be left to simmer for 8–10 hours while you get on with your life.

A slow cooker is ideal for families because the supper can be put on in the morning, after the children have gone to school, so that a warm, tasty meal is ready in the late afternoon or early evening, when you and the children are most tired. If you work unsocial hours or on shifts you can put on a

meal before you go to work, so that a meal is waiting when the rest of the family get home. Retired people can leave their supper to cook while they spend the day engaged in more rewarding activities.

Why slow cook?

Food that has been slowly cooked is packed with flavour. When microwave ovens first became widely available they captured everyone's imagination as the answer to our busy lives. But the reality is that food cooked in a microwave is often tasteless and lacking in colour, and most of us now use our microwave ovens for little more than defrosting and reheating foods.

Once a slow cooker is turned on, the food can be left to bubble gently, completely unattended. Because it cooks so slowly, there is no danger that the food will boil dry, spill over or burn on the bottom.

Foods from around the world

The recipes in this book have been inspired by foods from around the world, and they contain mellow spice blends from the Far East, India, Morocco and the Mediterranean and ingredients ranging from pesto, tamarind paste and harissa to aromatics, such as star anise, fennel, cumin and coriander, along with favourite flavourings, such as garlic, wine and fresh herbs.

There is something for everyone, from steaming bowls of soup to new family favourites such as Moroccan Seven Vegetable Stew (see page 140), Turkey Carbonnade with Polenta Squares (see page 102) and Summer Garden Pie (see page 103). For easy entertaining, why not try Peppered Venison

Fry foods first for added flavour when making a casserole or hotpot and always add boiling hot stock.

with Gorgonzola Scones (see page 108), Pot-roast Guinea Fowl with Salsa Verde (see page 116) or Feta Tiganito (see page 152)? As a finale, it would be hard to beat Sticky Toffee Apple Pudding (see page 200) or Mini Coffee Sponge Puddings with Coffee Liqueur (see page 224), with a soft, just melting chocolate centre. In summer you could offer Nectarine Compote with Orange Mascarpone (see page 210).

Not just for stews

A slow cooker is, of course, perfect for making slow-cooked meaty or vegetable casseroles, but it can also be used to steam puddings. The basin can be put directly on to the base of the slow cooker pot – there is no need for a trivet – and boiling water added to the pot until it comes halfway up the basin. Because there is no evaporation you will not need to remember to top up the water or return to find that the pot has boiled dry.

When water is added to the pot, a slow cooker can also be used as a bain marie or water bath to cook baked custards, pâtés or terrines. You can also pour alcoholic or fruit juice mixtures into the pot and heat them to make warming hot party punches or hot toddies, which can be ladled out of the slow cooker pot as required.

The slow cooker pot can also be used to make chocolate or cheese fondues, preserves, such as lemon curd or simple chutneys, and even to boil up bones or a chicken carcass to make into stock.

Money saving

Slow cookers use about the same amount of electricity as an electric light bulb, so they are cheap to run. Moreover, the long, slow cooking transforms even the toughest cheapest cuts of meat into dishes

You can make much more than just a casserole in a slow cooker. Use it as a steamer or water bath too.

that melt in the mouth, and the meat quite literally falls off the bone. Inexpensive dried beans, lentils and split peas also cook beautifully in tasty spiced or tomato sauces. Just remember to soak the beans and peas and boil them first.

Students in shared accommodation or young couples struggling with high mortgages will find slow cookers invaluable when trying to keep to a strict food budget. In addition, they are environmentally friendly: Why turn on the oven for just one dish when you can save on fuel by using the slow cooker?

Choose a medium-sized oval or round slow cooker if you are preparing meals for a family of four.

Getting started
Nothing could be easier than using a slow cooker, but if you are thinking of buying one for the first time, there are a few guidelines to bear in mind.

What size of slow cooker is best?
Slow cookers are measured by their total capacity, and there are three sizes. The size is usually printed on the packaging, together with the working capacity or the maximum space for food:

• For two people: a mini oval cooker with a maximum capacity of 1.5 litres (2½ pints) and a working capacity of 1 litre (1¾ pints).

• For four people: *either* a round *or* the more versatile oval cooker with a total capacity of 3.5 litres (6 pints) and a working capacity of 2.5 litres (4 pints).

• For six people: *either* a large oval cooker with a total capacity of 5 litres (8¾ pints) and a working capacity of 4 litres (7 pints) *or* the extra large round cooker with a total capacity of 6.5 litres (11½ pints) with a working capacity of 4.5 litres (8 pints).

Surprisingly, the very large slow cookers cost only a little more than the middle-sized models, and it is easy to be swept along, thinking that the larger cookers offer better value for money. Unless you have a big family or like to cook large quantities so that you have enough supper for one meal with extra portions to freeze, you will probably find that they are too big for your everyday needs.

The best and most versatile slow cooker is an oval one, which is ideal for cooking a whole chicken, has ample room for a pudding basin or four individual pudding moulds and is capacious enough to make soup for six portions.

Preheating your slow cooker
It is important to read the handbook that comes with your slow cooker before you begin cooking. Some manufacturers recommend preheating the cooker on the high setting for a minimum of 20 minutes before food is added. Others, however, recommend that the slow cooker is heated only when it is filled with food.

How full should the pot be?
A slow cooker pot must be used only when it contains liquid, and ideally it should be no less than half full. Aim for the three-quarter full mark, or, if you are making soups, make sure that the liquid is no higher than 2.5 cm (1 inch) from the top.

You need to half-fill a slow cooker when you are cooking meat, fish or vegetable dishes, but joints of meat should take up no more than two-thirds of the space. If you are using a pudding basin you must make sure that there is a 2 cm (¾ inch) space all the way round or, if you are using an oval slow cooker, 1 cm (½ inch) at the narrowest point.

Heat settings

All slow cookers will have 'high', 'low' and 'off' settings, and some models may also have 'medium', 'warm' or 'auto' setting. The high setting will generally take only half the time of the low setting when a diced meat or vegetable casserole is cooking. This can be useful if you plan to eat at lunchtime or get delayed in starting the casserole. Both settings will reach just below 100°C (212°F), or boiling point, during cooking, but this temperature is reached more quickly on the high setting.

Using a combination of settings can be very useful, and it is recommended by some manufacturers, especially at the beginning of cooking. If your slow cooker is very full, for example, cook on high for 30 minutes at the beginning of cooking to raise the temperature of the casserole quickly and then turn it to low for the remaining time. This can be done automatically if your model has an auto setting, when the cooker reduces the temperature automatically by means of a thermostat. This is ideal if you are rushing out to work.

Alternatively, increasing the temperature from low to high at the end of cooking can be useful if you want to thicken a casserole by reducing it down at the end of cooking, add cornflour, add extra green vegetables or reheat soups that you have puréed and returned to the pot.

The warm setting is suitable once the maximum cooking time has been reached, and it will keep the food 'on hold', which is useful if guests are late. The warm setting is not essential, however, because the low setting will not cause foods to spoil unless they are rice based.

What is best at what setting?

Low
- Diced meat or vegetable casseroles
- Chops or chicken joints
- Soups
- Egg custard desserts
- Rice dishes
- Fish dishes

High
- Sweet or savoury steamed puddings or sweet dishes that include a raising agent (self-raising flour or baking powder)
- Pâtés or terrines
- Whole chickens, guinea fowls or pheasants, gammon joints or half a shoulder of lamb

Timings

All the recipes in the book include a span of cooking times, which means that the dish will be tender and ready to eat at the lower time but can be left without spoiling for an extra hour or two, so there is no need to worry if you get delayed at work, stuck in traffic or bogged down in a do-it-yourself project.

If you want to speed up or slow down cooking times for diced meat or vegetable casseroles so that they fit around your plans better, adjust the heat settings and timings as suggested below:

Cook on Low	Cook on Medium	Cook on High
6–8 hours	4–6 hours	3–4 hours
8–10 hours	6–8 hours	5–6 hours
10–12 hours	8–10 hours	7–8 hours

Note: These timings were taken from the Morphy Richards slow cooker instruction handbook. Do not change timings or settings for fish, whole joints or dairy dishes.

Using your slow cooker for the first time

Before you start to use the slow cooker, put it on the work surface, somewhere out of the way, and make sure that the flex is tucked around the back of the machine and does not trail over the front of the work surface or near the hob.

The outside of the slow cooker does get hot, so warn all members of your family, and don't forget to use oven gloves when you are lifting the pot out of the housing. Carefully lift the slow cooker pot out of the housing and put it on to a heatproof mat on the table or work surface.

If your slow cooker lid has a vent in the top, make sure that the slow cooker is not put under an eye-level cupboard, or the steam may catch someone's arm as they reach into the cupboard.

Preparing food for the slow cooker

Meat

Slow-cooked meaty casseroles or stews are obvious choices for a slow cooker. There is no danger that the food will boil dry, and the lengthy cooking time means that the meat will be beautifully tender. For even cooking, make sure that all the pieces of meat are cut to the same size and press them below the surface of the liquid before cooking begins.

You can cook a whole chicken, guinea fowl or pheasant, even a small gammon joint or half a shoulder of lamb, in an oval slow cooker pot, but these should only be cooked on high, unlike diced meat or smaller chicken thigh or drumstick joints, which may be cooked on high, medium or low.

Fish

Fish can also be cooked in the slow cooker. Either cut it into pieces and bake in a rich tomato or vegetable sauce or poach a larger piece, such as a 500 g (1 lb) salmon fillet, in a wine and stock mixture. The slow, gentle cooking means that the fish will not break up or overcook. Make sure that the fish is covered by the liquid so that it cooks evenly.

Do not add shellfish until the last 15 minutes of cooking and make sure that the cooker is set to high. If you use frozen fish, make sure it has completely thawed before use.

Brown diced meat in a little oil or oil and butter to seal in the flavour before slow cooking.

Lower larger pieces of fish or pudding basins into the slow cooker using a long folded strip of foil.

Vegetables

Surprisingly, root vegetables can take longer to cook than meat. If you are adding them to a meaty casserole, make sure that you cut the vegetables into pieces that are a little smaller than the meat. Again, try to keep all the vegetable chunks the same size so that they cook evenly. Press the vegetables and the meat below the surface of the liquid before cooking commences.

Pasta and rice

Pasta tends to go soggy if it's added at the beginning of a recipe. For best results, cook the pasta separately in a saucepan of boiling water and mix it into the casserole just before serving. Small pasta shapes, such as macaroni or shells, can be added to soups 30–45 minutes before the end of cooking.

Basmati and ordinary white long-grain rice can be used in slow cookers, but you will get better results with easy-cook rice, which has been partially cooked during manufacture. Some of the starch has been

washed off, making it less sticky when cooked. Allow a minimum of 250 ml (8 fl oz) water for each 100 g (3½ oz) of easy-cook rice or up to 500 ml (17 fl oz) for risotto rice.

Pulses and lentils

Dried pulses must be soaked overnight in plenty of cold water before use. Drain them, then put them in a saucepan with fresh water and bring to the boil. Boil rapidly for 10 minutes, then drain or add with the cooking liquid to the slow cooker (see the individual recipes for details). Pearl barley and red, Puy or green lentils do not need soaking overnight, but if you are unsure, always check the instructions on the packet.

Cream and milk

Cream and milk can be added but generally only at the beginning of cooking in rice pudding or baked egg custard dishes. Use full-fat milk or double cream because they are less likely to separate.

If you are making soup add the milk at the very end, after the soup has been puréed. Stir cream into soups just 15 minutes before the end of cooking or swirl it over the soup before serving.

Thickening stews and casseroles

Casseroles can be thickened in the same ways as if you were cooking conventionally. Add the flour after searing meat or frying onions, then gradually mix in the stock. Alternatively, add cornflour mixed with a little water 30–60 minutes before the end of cooking or pour off the liquid from the cooked dish into a pan and boil it on the hob until reduced.

Because the liquid does not evaporate during cooking, as it would on the hob, there is no need to lift the lid and check on a stew's progress or top up with stock during cooking. You may find that you can use slightly less stock than you would normally do, but remember that it is important that the meat or vegetables are covered with stock so that they cook evenly.

Getting organized

If you plan to switch on the slow cooker before you go out to work in the morning, you may find it helpful to semi-prepare the dish to be cooked the night before. Chop the onion and seal it in a small plastic bag. Put diced vegetables in an airtight plastic container with a little water, then use this water to add to the slow cooker pot. Dice or slice meat and wrap it in clingfilm or kitchen foil.

Keep all the foods in the refrigerator, then brown them in the morning, while the slow cooker heats up, if your model requires this. Add boiling water to a low-salt stock cube with any vegetable soaking liquid or heat up the stock in the frying pan, after sealing the meat. Transfer the ingredients to the slow cooker pot, add the lid to cover and leave to cook while you are out.

In most of the savoury recipes in this book the ingredients are browned first in a frying pan to improve both their appearance and taste, then thickened, either with flour before they are added to the slow cooker pot or with a little cornflour at the end of cooking.

If you prefer to skip the browning stage, simply add the diced, sliced or minced meat or chicken pieces straight from the refrigerator to the slow cooker pot and cover with boiling stock. You will need to increase the minimum cooking time, adding an extra 2–3 hours if cooking the food on low. Do not be tempted to lift the lid during the first half of cooking or you will need to add an extra 20 minutes to the cooking time. Thicken the casserole at the end with a little cornflour mixed to a paste with water, then cook on high for 30 minutes.

Whether or not you brown the ingredients first, make sure you always add **hot** liquid to the pot.

Do I need any special equipment?

You will probably already have all the equipment you need, although if you are buying a new slow cooker why not treat yourself to a new nonstick frying pan for preparing foods before slow cooking?

It's likely that you will already have a 1.25 litre (2¼ pint) basin for steamed puddings, such as the

You may find that you use slightly less stock as there is no risk of evaporation or the stew boiling dry.

Rosemary Pudding with Mushrooms and Chestnuts (see page 154) or Rum and Raisin Spotted Dick (see page 202). If you have one that is slightly larger, use this, but check that it will fit in your slow cooker before you begin. For recipes such as Bobotie (see page 66), Sticky Toffee Apple Pudding (see page 200), Sticky Glazed Banana Gingerbread (see page 218) or Marbled Chocolate and Vanilla Cheesecake (see page 215) you will need either a soufflé-style dish that is 14 cm (5½ inches) across and 9 cm (3½ inches) high or a straight-sided round dish with a capacity of 1.25 litres (2¼ pints).

The individual puddings, such as the Black Cherry and Chocolate Puddings (see page 204) or the Mini Coffee Sponge Puddings with Coffee Liqueur (see page 224), will require four individual metal moulds, each with a capacity of 200 ml (7 fl oz). Small coffee cups also make good moulds for the Lemon Custard Creams (see page 216), and six cups will fit snugly side by side in an oval slow cooker pot. Again, check that your chosen containers will fit inside your slow cooker before you begin.

Adapting your own recipes

If you want to try some of your own favourite recipes in your slow cooker, you should first look at a similar recipe in this book to give you an idea of the quantity that will fit in the slow cooker pot and the appropriate timing for the main ingredient. Because a slow cooker cooks food gently and evenly you will almost certainly need to reduce the amount of liquid. Begin by using just half the amount of hot liquid specified in the original recipe and then increase it as needed, pressing foods beneath the surface of the liquid and upping the amount as required until they are just covered. Recipes that contain fresh tomatoes will turn to pulp during cooking, so you will not need quite so much liquid.

The steam condenses on the lid of the slow cooker and returns to the pot so there is no danger that food will boil dry. If you find you have reduced the amount of liquid too much, add a little more boiling stock or water at the end of cooking to compensate.

Tip

- **To lift a hot basin easily out of the slow cooker you can buy macramé string pudding basin bags, but do make sure that they will fit a 1.25 litre (2¼ pint) basin before you buy. Alternatively, tear off two long pieces of foil. Fold each into thirds to make a long, narrow strap. Lay one on top of the other to make a cross, then sit the pudding basin in the centre. Lift up the straps and carefully lower the basin into the slow cooker pot.**

It is usually best to add milk or cream at the end of the recipe unless the recipe uses the slow cooker pot as a bain marie or water bath with hot water poured around a cooking dish. Rice pudding is the exception to this rule, and you should use full-fat milk and not semi-skimmed or skimmed milk. Refer to individual recipes in the book for guidance.

Changing the recipes to suit a smaller or larger slow cooker

All the recipes in this book have been tested in a standard slow cooker with a total capacity of 3.5 litres (6 pints). Larger 5 litre (8¾ pint), six-portion sized cookers or tiny 1.5 litre (2½ pint), two-person cookers are also available. To adapt the recipes in this book simply halve for two portions or add half as much again to the recipe, keeping the timings the same. All the recipes made in pudding basins, soufflé dishes or individual moulds may also be cooked in a larger slow cooker for the same amount of time.

Using the slow cooker in conjunction with a freezer

Most of the soups and stews in this book may be frozen, and if you live on your own, freezing individual portions can be a great time saver. After all, it takes little extra effort to make a casserole for four than for two. Defrost portions in the refrigerator overnight or at room temperature for 4 hours, then reheat thoroughly in a saucepan on the hob or in the microwave on full power.

Quick tips

• You can make so much more than casseroles in the slow cooker. Try steamed puddings, baked custards, hot toddies, even cakes, chutneys and preserves.

• Always check that the joint, pudding basin, soufflé dish or individual moulds will fit into your slow cooker pot before you begin to prepare the ingredients to avoid later frustration.

• Foods cooked in a slow cooker must contain some liquid.

• If you have an electric hand blender, you can purée soups while they are still in the slow cooker pot, but take care that you do not knock the edges of the pot as it will become damaged quickly.

• Foods will not brown during cooking, so lift the slow cooker pot out of the housing and transfer it to a preheated grill or oven with a grill element. Alternatively, use a cook's blowtorch if you have one.

• Don't be tempted to keep lifting the lid and stirring the food while it is cooking in the slow cooker. Because the food only bubbles gently, even on the highest setting, there is no need to make sure it is not sticking, burning or boiling over. **Every time you lift the lid you add 20 minutes to the cooking time.**

• Bear in mind that the smaller the pieces of food, the quicker they will cook. So, if you are leaving the meal to cook all day while you are at work, it's fine to use big, chunky pieces of meat and vegetables.

• If you are going to freeze all or part of the meal, remove it from the slow cooker and place in a heatproof container to cool down; it will not cool down quickly enough if simply left in the pot.

• Always follow the recipe carefully. Some ingredients need to be added in a specific order to allow for accurate cooking times. Food at the bottom of the cooker will cook faster, so certain ingredients will benefit from being added first.

• Use your slow cooker to use up odds and ends of vegetables and pulses. You can make delicious stews or soups with just about any vegetables and extra flavours can be added by using spices. It is also a great way to make healthy, hearty meals for babies and toddlers. Large batches can be made in one session and frozen in individual portions. The lengthy cooking time means that the food will be very tender and easy for little ones to eat.

• Fat tends to melt if cooked for long periods of time so trim away excess fat from meat and remove the skin from chicken breasts and thighs before cooking.

Keep safe

• If you are using dried beans, always soak them overnight in cold water and boil them rapidly in a saucepan of fresh water for 10 minutes before you add them to the slow cooker pot. Lentils do not need pre-soaking or boiling.

• Always make sure that frozen food is thawed thoroughly before you add it to the slow cooker, although some frozen vegetables, such as peas and broad beans, can be added without thawing.

• Raw foods that have been taken out of the freezer, thawed and cooked in the slow cooker pot can be returned to the freezer once cooled.

• Add well-rinsed shellfish at the end of cooking in the slow cooker and cook the mixture on high for 15 minutes to make sure that it is piping hot.

• If you are cooking a joint of meat, make sure that it does not fill more than the lower two-thirds of the slow cooker pot. Completely cover the meat with hot liquid. Always check that the joint of meat is fully cooked before serving, either by using a meat thermometer or by inserting a skewer through the thickest part of the joint or through the thickest part of the leg into the breast if you are cooking a whole chicken, guinea fowl or pheasant. The juices will run clear when the meat is ready.

As the slow cooker heats up it forms a water seal just under the lid. Lifting the lid adds 20 minutes to the cooking time.

• Remove the slow cooker pot from the housing when the food is cooked and then serve. Leftover food should be transferred to a plastic container, covered and allowed to cool at room temperature before being chilled in the refrigerator.

• Never reheat cooked food in a slow cooker. Reheat a cooked casserole in a saucepan on the hob and make sure that you bring it to the boil and cook it through thoroughly. Only reheat cooked food once.

• Never try to repair an electrical fault yourself – contact the manufacturer for advice.

Cooker care & cleaning

After use, make sure that your slow cooker is switched off, both on the control panel and at the electric socket outlet, and preferably keep it unplugged. In no circumstances should you attempt to clean any part of the cooker until it has cooled down completely. Similarly, do not pack it away in a cupboard until completely cold. Refer to the following guidelines for cleaning your cooker, but do verify with your manufacturer's specific instructions. Ensure

Slow cookers are easy to care for – simply wipe the cooled slow cooker base after use and remember never to immerse the base unit in water.

that the plug and electrical connections remain dry at all times.

Wash the slow cooker lid and ceramic pot in warm soapy water. If your lid has an air vent make sure it is free from any pieces of food. Dislodge any food stains with a washing-up brush. Some manufacturers say that the cooker pot may be washed in a dishwasher, but do check your instruction manual first.

For stubborn stains fill the slow cooker pot with warm soapy water but do not immerse the outside of the pot in water – the base is porous and will absorb water and may crack when next used in the slow cooker.

Wipe the outside of the cooker and buff up with a tea towel or kitchen paper. Do not use abrasive cleaner, especially if the cooker has a chrome finish. Wipe the inside of the cooker and, if it gets very dirty after prolonged use, use a little cream cleaner on a wrung-out dish cloth then dry with kitchen paper.

Slow cooker sense

- The outside of the slow cooker gets hot when it is switched on, so make sure that younger members of the family know not to touch it

- Never cook food directly inside the base unit, always use the ceramic cooker pot

- Make sure the flex does not trail over the work surface or near the hob

- If the lid has a steam vent, make sure that the slow cooker is not sited beneath an eye level cupboard or someone may scald themselves when reaching into the cupboard

- Never immerse the slow cooker in water

Cooking stocks in a slow cooker

All meals prepared in a slow cooker require liquid to be added and, although water is often used, there are often occasions when a stock is required. A homemade stock is always preferable to a stock cube and can be made in batches and frozen until needed. A slow cooker is ideal for making stocks, as they require lengthy cooking times in order to release all the flavours.

Making stock is a great way to get the most from a chicken.

Vegetable Stock

Preparation time: 10 minutes
Cooking time: 10 hours
Cooking temperature: low
Slow cooker size: standard

2 small onions, peeled and sliced
2 carrots, peeled and chopped
2 celery stalks, chopped
1 medium leek, trimmed and chopped
2 garlic cloves, halved
8 black peppercorns
2 bay leaves
Small bunch of parsley stalks

1 Put all the ingredients in the slow cooker then top up with water. Don't fill the cooker right to the top with water, as the vegetables will release moisture when they cook, so there needs to be space for this. Cook for 10 hours on low.

2 Strain the stock into a large, heatproof container to cool.

3 Either store the stock in the refrigerator and use it within 3 days, or freeze it in smaller portions for later use.

Chicken Stock

Preparation time: 10 minutes
Cooking time: 10 hours
Cooking temperature: low
Slow cooker size: standard

1 chicken carcass
2 small onions, peeled and sliced
2 carrots, peeled and chopped
2 celery stalks, chopped
1 medium leek, trimmed and chopped
2 small thyme sprigs
4 garlic cloves, left unpeeled
Small bunch of parsley stalks

1 Chop the chicken carcass into pieces, or leave it whole, depending on the size and shape of your slow cooker. Put the ingredients in the slow cooker and top up with water, ensuring all the ingredients are covered. Cook for 10 hours on low.

2 Strain the stock well and transfer to a heatproof container to cool.

3 Either store the stock in the refrigerator and use it within 3 days, or freeze it in smaller portions for later use.

Soups & starters

Celeriac soup

with Roquefort toasts

This velvety smooth soup is topped with slices of toasted French bread and Roquefort cheese. A greatly underrated vegetable, celeriac has a more delicate flavour than celery.

Serves 6

Preparation time: 30 minutes
Cooking time: 6¼–7¼ hours
Cooking temperature: low and high
Slow cooker size: standard

1 tablespoon sunflower oil
1 large onion, chopped
25 g (1 oz) butter
625 g (1¼ lb) celeriac, peeled and diced
750 ml (1¼ pints) hot vegetable or chicken stock
salt and pepper

To finish

300 ml (½ pint) milk
12 thin slices of French bread
100 g (3½ oz) Roquefort cheese
150 ml (¼ pint) double cream
small bunch of chives

1 Preheat the slow cooker if necessary – see manufacturer's instructions. Heat the oil in a frying pan, add the onion and fry, stirring, for 5 minutes until softened. Add the butter and celeriac and fry for 5 more minutes.

2 Transfer the vegetables to the slow cooker pot, add the hot stock and salt and pepper and mix together. Cover with the lid and cook on low for 6–7 hours.

3 To finish the soup, ladle the celeriac mixture into a food processor or blender and blend in batches until smooth. Turn the cooker setting to high and return the puréed soup to the slow cooker pot. Stir in the milk and reheat for 15 minutes.

4 Just before serving, toast the French bread on both sides under a preheated grill. Top with crumbled cheese and return to the grill until just bubbling. Stir the cream into the soup, chop half the chives and mix into the soup, then ladle the soup into individual bowls. Float the cheese toasts on the soup and sprinkle with long pieces of chives.

Tips
- **Strips of Parma ham can be added to the toasts before the cheese.**
- **The soup freezes well without the cream and toast topping.**

Cajun red bean soup

Serves 6

Preparation time: 25 minutes, plus overnight soaking
Cooking time: 8½–10½ hours
Cooking temperature: low
Slow cooker size: standard

125 g (4 oz) dried red kidney beans, soaked
  overnight in cold water
2 tablespoons sunflower oil
1 large onion, chopped
1 red pepper, halved, cored, de-seeded and diced
1 carrot, diced
1 baking potato, diced
2–3 garlic cloves, chopped (optional)
2 teaspoons mixed Cajun spice
400 g (13 oz) can chopped tomatoes
1 tablespoon brown sugar
1 litre (1¾ pints) hot vegetable stock
50 g (2 oz) okra, sliced
50 g (2 oz) green beans, thinly sliced
salt and pepper
crusty bread, to serve

1 Preheat the slow cooker if necessary – see manufacturer's instructions. Drain and rinse the soaked beans, add to a saucepan, cover with fresh water and bring to the boil. Boil vigorously for 10 minutes.

2 Meanwhile, heat the oil in a large frying pan. Add the onion and fry, stirring, for 5 minutes until softened. Add the red pepper, carrot, potato and garlic, if using, and fry for 2–3 minutes. Stir in the mixed Cajun spice, canned tomatoes, sugar and plenty of salt and pepper and bring to the boil.

3 Transfer the mixture to the slow cooker pot, add the drained beans and hot stock and mix together. Cover with the lid and cook on low for 8–10 hours.

4 Add the sliced green vegetables, replace the lid and cook for 30 minutes. Ladle the soup into bowls and serve with crusty bread.

Tips
• **Always boil soaked dried red kidney beans rapidly in a saucepan of boiling water for 10 minutes, before adding to the slow cooker pot, to ensure that their toxins are removed.**

• **If mixed Cajun spice is unavailable, use chilli powder instead, but reduce the quantity to suit your taste.**

Gingered carrot soup

Give home-made carrot soup an extra zing with ginger. Fresh root ginger has a far more intense flavour than powdered ginger and can be stored for several weeks in the salad drawer of the refrigerator. This soup freezes well.

Serves 6
Preparation time: 30 minutes
Cooking time: 4¼–5¼ hours
Cooking temperature: low
Slow cooker size: standard

1 tablespoon sunflower oil
15 g (½ oz) butter
1 large onion, finely chopped
500 g (1 lb) carrots, diced
75 g (3 oz) red lentils
3.5 cm (1½ inch) piece of root ginger, peeled
   and finely chopped
3 teaspoons mild curry paste
1.2 litres (2 pints) hot chicken or vegetable stock
300 ml (½ pint) full-fat milk
salt and pepper
coriander sprigs, to garnish

1 Preheat the slow cooker if necessary – see manufacturer's instructions. Heat the oil and butter in a frying pan. Add the onion and fry, stirring, for 5 minutes until pale golden.

2 Transfer the onion to the slow cooker pot and add the carrots, lentils and ginger. Mix the curry paste into the hot stock, pour into the pot and season well with salt and pepper. Stir together then cover with the lid and cook on low for 4–5 hours.

3 The soup can be left chunky at this stage or puréed in a food processor or blender, in batches until smooth. Stir in the milk, cook for 15 minutes until heated through then ladle into individual bowls and garnish with coriander.

Salmon chowder

This chunky soup is served topped with a tangy lime and chilli butter. Cod, haddock or a mixture of plain and smoked fish can be used instead of salmon if preferred.

Serves 6

Preparation time: 30 minutes
Cooking time: 3 hours 10 minutes–3 hours 40 minutes
Cooking temperature: low
Slow cooker size: standard

1 tablespoon sunflower oil
1 large onion, roughly chopped
2 potatoes, about 300 g (10 oz), finely diced
1 fennel bulb
750 ml (1¼ pints) fish stock
300 ml (½ pint) milk
300 g (10 oz) salmon fillet, skinned and cut
   into 2 pieces
150 ml (¼ pint) single cream
small bunch of parsley or chives, roughly chopped
salt and pepper
crusty bread, to serve

Lime and chilli butter

½–1 large mild red chilli, halved,
   deseeded and finely chopped
75 g (3 oz) butter, at room temperature
grated rind and juice of 1 lime
pepper

Tip
- **Always wash your hands well after handling chillies as they can make your eyes sting if you touch them without thinking.**

1 Preheat the slow cooker if necessary – see manufacturer's instructions. Heat the oil in a frying pan, add the onion and fry, stirring, for 5 minutes until softened but not browned. Add the potatoes and cook for 3 minutes.

2 Meanwhile, cut the green feathery tops off the fennel and reserve. Cut the vegetable in half, cut away the core then finely chop. Add the chopped fennel, stock and salt and pepper to the frying pan and bring to the boil.

3 Transfer the mixture to the slow cooker pot. Cover with the lid and cook on low for 2½–3 hours until the potato is tender. Meanwhile, make the lime and chilli butter: beat the chopped chilli into the butter with the lime rind and a little pepper. Gradually mix in the lime juice then chill well.

4 Stir the milk into the chowder then add the salmon pieces. Replace the lid and cook for 30 minutes until the salmon flakes easily when pressed with a knife. Lift it out with a slotted spoon, put on a plate and flake into chunky pieces using a knife and fork, carefully removing any bones. Return the salmon to the soup with the cream, green fennel tops and herbs. Taste and adjust the seasoning. Cook for 10 minutes more.

5 Ladle the chowder into individual bowls and top with spoonfuls of the lime and chilli butter.

with lime & chilli butter

Cock-a-leekie soup

A traditional chicken and leek soup is given an unusual topping of oven-baked, crispy, flaky, thyme- and salt-flavoured pastry shapes. Serve the soup with warmed bread rolls or traditional fried bread croutons instead of the pastry croutes if preferred.

Serves 6

Preparation time: 35 minutes
Cooking time: 4¼–6¼ hours
Cooking temperature: low
Slow cooker size: standard

2 leeks, about 500 g (1 lb), trimmed and cleaned
25 g (1 oz) butter
1 tablespoon sunflower oil
4 boneless, skinless chicken thighs, diced
1 potato, about 250 g (8 oz), diced
1 litre (1¾ pints) hot chicken stock
65 g (2½ oz) pitted prunes
salt and pepper

Croutes

1 ready-rolled puff pastry sheet from a 425 g (14 oz)
   packet of 2, defrosted if frozen
1 egg, beaten
salt flakes
a few thyme sprigs

1 Preheat the slow cooker if necessary – see manufacturer's instructions. Thinly slice the leeks and separate the green slices from the white.

2 Heat the butter and oil in a frying pan, add the diced chicken and fry for 5 minutes, stirring until browned. Add the white sliced leek and potato and fry for 2 more minutes.

3 Transfer the chicken and leek mixture to the slow cooker pot. Pour in the stock then stir in the prunes and a little salt and pepper. Cover with the lid and cook on low for 4–6 hours.

4 When almost ready to serve, stir the reserved green leek into the soup and cook for 15 minutes. Meanwhile, unroll the pastry sheet and cut out 7.5 cm (3 inch) circles. Cut these in half then arrange the semi-circles on a moistened baking sheet and brush with the beaten egg. Sprinkle with a few salt flakes and the torn leaves from the thyme sprigs. Bake in a preheated oven, 200°C (400°F), Gas Mark 6, for 7–8 minutes until well risen and golden.

5 Ladle the soup into individual bowls and serve topped with the pastry croutes.

Mujaddarah

Serves 6

Preparation time: 30 minutes
Cooking time: 3½–4 hours
Cooking temperature: low
Slow cooker size: standard

1 tablespoon olive oil
1 large onion, chopped
1 teaspoon cumin seeds, roughly crushed
2 teaspoons coriander seeds, roughly crushed
2–3 garlic cloves, chopped
¼ teaspoon ground cinnamon
400 g (13 oz) can chopped tomatoes
2 teaspoons soft light or dark brown sugar
600 ml (1 pint) hot vegetable stock
175 g (6 oz) green lentils
100 g (3½ oz) easy-cook brown rice
salt and pepper

To serve
1 tablespoon olive oil
1 large onion, thinly sliced
small bunch of coriander or mint leaves, torn
150 g (5 oz) natural yogurt

1 Preheat the slow cooker if necessary – see manufacturer's instructions. Heat the oil in a large frying pan, add the onion and fry, stirring, for 5 minutes until softened.

2 Stir the crushed cumin and coriander seeds into the onion with the garlic and cinnamon. Add the canned tomatoes, sugar and plenty of salt and pepper and bring to the boil, stirring.

3 Transfer the tomato mixture to the slow cooker pot then stir in the hot stock, lentils and rice. Cover with the lid and cook on low for 3½–4 hours, stirring once or twice, until the rice and lentils are tender.

4 When almost ready to serve, heat the 1 tablespoon oil in a frying pan, add the sliced onion and fry for 8–10 minutes until golden brown. Spoon the lentil mixture in bowls, top with the fried onion, torn herb leaves and spoonfuls of yogurt.

Tip

• **Stir the mixture once or twice during cooking and make sure that the rice is below the surface of the liquid at all times or it will taste very dry and crisp.**

Salmon

This quick and easy soup is flavoured with miso, a Japanese paste made from fermented soya beans. You can also add mirin, a Japanese cooking wine made from rice.

Serves 6

Preparation time: 15 minutes
Cooking time: 1 hour 40 minutes–2 hours 10 minutes
Cooking temperature: low and high
Slow cooker size: standard

4 salmon steaks, about 125 g (4 oz) each
1 carrot, thinly sliced
4 spring onions, thinly sliced
4 cup mushrooms, about 125 g (4 oz) in total,
   thinly sliced
1 large red chilli, halved, deseeded and finely chopped
2 cm (¾ inch) fresh root ginger, peeled and finely
   chopped
3 tablespoons miso
1 tablespoon dark soy sauce
2 tablespoons mirin (optional)
1.2 litres (2 pints) hot fish stock
75 g (3 oz) mangetout, thinly sliced
coriander leaves, to garnish

1 Preheat the slow cooker if necessary – see manufacturer's instructions. Rinse the salmon in cold water, drain and place in the slow cooker pot. Put the carrot, spring onions, mushrooms, chilli and ginger on top of the fish.

2 Add the miso, soy sauce and mirin, if using, to the hot stock and stir until the miso has dissolved. Pour the stock mixture over the salmon and vegetables and cover.

3 Cook on low for 1½–2 hours or until the fish is tender and the soup is piping hot. Lift the fish out with a slotted spoon and transfer it to a plate. Flake it into chunky pieces, discarding the skin and any bones.

4 Return the fish to the slow cooker pot and add the mangetout. Cook on high for 10 minutes or until the mangetout are just tender, then ladle the soup into bowls and serve topped with coriander leaves.

Tip
• **Miso and mirin are available from most larger supermarkets and from specialist oriental stores. Once opened, store miso in the refrigerator.**

in hot miso broth

Beetroot & carrot

A favourite in eastern European countries, this deep red broth is flavoured with beef stock. Vegetarians could use vegetable stock and add some dried mushrooms for extra flavour.

Serves 6

Preparation time: 25 minutes
Cooking time: 7¼–8¼ hours
Cooking temperature: low and high
Slow cooker size: standard

25 g (1 oz) butter
1 tablespoon sunflower oil
1 large onion, finely chopped
375 g (12 oz) raw beetroot, trimmed, peeled
  and diced
2 carrots, diced
250 g (8 oz) potatoes, diced
2 garlic cloves, finely chopped
1 litre (1¾ pint) hot beef stock
1 tablespoon tomato purée
2 bay leaves
2 celery sticks, diced (optional)
125 g (4 oz) red cabbage, finely shredded
salt and pepper

To serve

2 tablespoons red wine vinegar
1 tablespoon caster sugar
300 ml (½ pint) hot beef stock

To garnish

150 ml (¼ pint) double cream
coarsely ground black pepper

1 Preheat the slow cooker if necessary – see manufacturer's instructions. Heat the butter and oil in a large frying pan, add the onion and fry, stirring, for 5 minutes or until softened. Stir in the beetroot, carrots, potatoes and garlic and fry for 2 minutes.

2 Stir in the stock (or as much as you can get in the pan), tomato purée, bay leaves and salt and pepper and bring to the boil, stirring.

3 Put the celery, if using, and red cabbage in the slow cooker pot. Pour over the hot stock mixture (reheat any stock that would not fit into the pan at the beginning and add it to the pot when it is boiling), cover and cook on low for 7–8 hours or until tender.

4 Stir in the vinegar and sugar then purée the soup in batches in a liquidizer or food processor until smooth then return it to the slow cooker. Mix in the extra hot stock and reheat on high for 15 minutes. Ladle the soup into bowls and spoon a little cream over the top of each and sprinkle with a little pepper.

soup with cream

Chunky pistou
with Parmesan thins

Serves 6

Preparation time: 25 minutes
Cooking time: 6 hours 15 minutes–8 hours 20 minutes
Cooking temperature: low and high
Slow cooker size: standard

1 tablespoon olive oil
1 onion, finely chopped
1 baking potato, diced
1 carrot, diced
2 garlic cloves, finely chopped
410 g (13¼ oz) can haricot beans, drained
1.2 litres (2 pints) hot chicken or vegetable stock
2 teaspoons pesto, plus extra to serve
100 g (3½ oz) broccoli, cut into small florets,
   stems sliced
100 g (3½ oz) green beans, each cut into 4 slices
2 tomatoes, diced
100 g (3½ oz) Parmesan cheese, coarsely grated
salt and pepper
bunch of basil, to garnish (optional)

1 Preheat the slow cooker if necessary – see manufacturer's instructions. Heat the oil in a large frying pan, add the onion and fry, stirring, for 5 minutes or until lightly browned. Add the potato, carrot and garlic and cook for 2 minutes.

2 Transfer the vegetable mixture to the slow cooker pot, add the haricot beans, hot stock and pesto. Season to taste with salt and pepper, mix thoroughly, cover and cook on low for 6–8 hours.

3 Add the broccoli, green beans and tomatoes, replace the lid and cook on high for 15–20 minutes or until the vegetables are tender.

4 Meanwhile, line a large baking sheet with nonstick baking paper and sprinkle the Parmesan into 18 mounds, leaving space between them for the cheese to spread. Cook in a preheated oven, 190°C, 375°F, Gas Mark 5, for about 5 minutes or until the cheese has melted and is just beginning to brown around the edges. Leave to cool and harden, then peel away the paper.

5 Ladle the soup into bowls, top with extra spoonfuls of pesto, some basil leaves, if liked, and the Parmesan thins.

Lamb hotchpot

This traditional favourite is made with a clear broth speckled with root vegetables and thickened with pearl barley. You can vary the vegetables depending on what's in season; it is very good with diced parsnips or turnip.

Serves 6

Preparation time: 20 minutes
Cooking time: 8¼–10¼ hours
Cooking temperature: low and high
Slow cooker size: standard

15 g (½ oz) butter
1 tablespoon sunflower oil
1 large onion, finely chopped
400 g (13 oz) lamb fillet, diced
175 g (6 oz) carrots, diced
175 g (6 oz) swedes, diced
200 g (7 oz) potatoes, diced
1 leek, thinly sliced (keep white and green slices separate)
50 g (2 oz) pearl barley
2–3 sprigs fresh or a little dried rosemary
1.5 litre (2½ pints) lamb stock
salt and pepper
warm bread, to serve

1 Preheat the slow cooker if necessary – see manufacturer's instructions. Heat the butter and oil in a saucepan, add the onion and lamb and cook over a high heat until the lamb is browned and the onion is golden.

2 Stir in the carrots, swedes, potatoes, white sliced leek, pearl barley and rosemary. Add the stock, (or as much as you can get in the pan), season to taste with salt and pepper and bring to the boil.

3 Transfer the mixture to the slow cooker pot, (bring any remaining stock to the boil and add to the pot) cover and cook on low for 8–10 hours or until the pearl barley, vegetables and lamb are tender.

4 Add the green sliced leek tops and cook on high for 15 minutes. Ladle the broth into bowls and serve with warm bread.

Tips

• **This soup freezes well, either in individual-sized plastic boxes or plastic bags or in a larger, family-sized container. Microwave or reheat in a saucepan.**

• **For a really filling meal, add small herby dumplings at the same time as the green sliced leeks and cook them for 30 minutes.**

Caldo verde

A favourite Portuguese rustic soup, this is flavoured with diced chorizo sausage and potato. It's almost a meal in itself if it's served with chunks of warm, crusty bread.

Serves 6

Preparation time: 20 minutes
Cooking time: 6 hours 15 minutes–8 hours 20 minutes
Cooking temperature: low and high
Slow cooker size: standard

2 tablespoons olive oil
2 onions, chopped
2 garlic cloves, finely chopped
150 g (5 oz) chorizo sausage, skinned and diced
625 g (1¼ lb) or 3 small baking potatoes, diced into 1 cm (½ inch) cubes
1 teaspoon *picante pimentón* (Spanish hot smoked paprika)
1.2 litres (2 pints) hot chicken stock
125 g (4 oz) green cabbage, finely shredded
salt and pepper
warm crusty bread, to serve

1 Preheat the slow cooker if necessary – see manufacturer's instructions. Heat the oil in a large frying pan, add the onions and fry, stirring, for 5 minutes or until lightly browned. Add the garlic, chorizo, potatoes and *picante pimenton* and cook for 2 minutes.

2 Transfer the mixture to the slow cooker pot, add the hot stock and season to taste with salt and pepper. Cover and cook on low for 6–8 hours.

3 Add the cabbage, replace the lid and cook on high for 15–20 minutes or until the cabbage is tender. Ladle the soup into bowls and serve with warm, crusty bread.

> **Tip**
> • If you are using stock cubes, make up the quantity for this soup with 2 cubes in boiling water. Avoid cubes that are highly seasoned or they will overpower the flavour of the chorizo.

Smoked gammon

& mixed bean chowder

If you prefer, a small knuckle joint instead of a smoked gammon joint would work equally well in this filling soup.

Serves 6
Preparation time: 20 minutes, plus soaking
Cooking time: 6–7 hours
Cooking temperature: high
Slow cooker size: standard

500 g (1 lb) boneless smoked gammon joint
150 g (5 oz) country soup mix (blend of dried
    peas, barley, lentils and beans)
2 onions, roughly chopped
1 carrot, diced
1 bay leaf
4 cloves
1.5 litres (2½ pints) vegetable stock
pepper
chopped flat leaf parsley, to garnish
warm crusty bread, to serve

1 Put the gammon joint in a bowl, cover with cold water and transfer to the refrigerator. Put the soup mixture in a separate bowl, cover with cold water and leave at room temperature. Leave both to soak overnight.

2 Preheat the slow cooker if necessary – see manufacturer's instructions. Drain the bean mixture and put it in a saucepan with the onions, carrot, bay leaf, cloves, stock and pepper. Bring to the boil and boil rapidly for 10 minutes, skimming off any scum.

3 Remove the gammon from the soaking water and put it in the slow cooker pot. Top with the bean and stock mixture, cover and cook on high for 6–7 hours or until well cooked.

4 Lift the gammon out of the slow cooker pot, cut away the rind and any fat and break the meat into bite-sized pieces. Return the meat to the slow cooker pot and sprinkle with parsley. Ladle the soup into bowls and serve with warm crusty bread.

Tips
- **If you can't find a small gammon joint, cut off thin slices from a larger piece until the joint will fit into your slow cooker. Grill the slices and serve them with poached eggs and chips for a quick supper or brunch.**
- **If your slow cooker is on the small side, keep back 300 ml (½ pint) stock and add it once you take the gammon joint out at the end.**
- **Warn diners to look out for the cloves.**

Creamy cauliflower with honey cashews

Serves 6

Preparation time: 30 minutes
Cooking time: 4¼–5¼ hours
Cooking temperature: low and high
Slow cooker size: standard

25 g (1 oz) butter
1 tablespoon olive oil
1 onion, roughly chopped
50 g (2 oz) cashew nuts
750 ml (1¼ pints) vegetable stock
grated nutmeg, to taste
1 large cauliflower, cut into florets and
  woody core discarded
450 ml (¾ pint) full-fat milk
150 ml (¼ pint) double cream
salt and pepper

Caramelized cashew nuts
15 g (½ oz) butter
50 g (2 oz) cashew nuts
1 tablespoon set honey

1 Preheat the slow cooker if necessary – see manufacturer's instructions. Heat the butter and oil in a large frying pan, add the onion and 50 g (2 oz) cashew nuts and fry until just beginning to colour. Add the stock, a little nutmeg and salt and pepper and bring to the boil.

2 Put the cauliflower in the slow cooker pot, add the hot onion mixture, cover and cook on low for 4–5 hours or until the cauliflower is tender.

3 Meanwhile, make the caramelized cashew nuts. Heat the butter in a clean frying pan, add the nuts and cook until they are pale golden. Add the honey and bubble for 1–2 minutes or until the nuts are deep golden and the honey has darkened slightly. Tip on to a baking sheet lined with oiled foil, leave to cool and harden, then break into pieces.

4 Purée the soup in batches in a liquidizer or food processor until smooth. Return it to the slow cooker, stir in the milk and half the cream. Add a little more nutmeg and salt and pepper if wished, then cook on high for 15 minutes or until reheated.

5 Ladle the soup into bowls, swirl the remaining cream over the top and garnish with broken pieces of the caramelized cashew nuts.

Tip
• **If you prefer, use maple syrup instead of honey to caramelize the cashew nuts.**

Parsnip soup with chilli & Stilton

Serves 6

Preparation time: 35 minutes
Cooking time: 4¼–5¼ hours
Cooking temperature: low and high
Slow cooker size: standard

25 g (1 oz) butter
1 tablespoon sunflower oil
1 onion, chopped
625 g (1¼ lb) parsnips, diced
1 cooking apple, about 250 g (8 oz), quartered,
  cored, peeled and diced
1½ teaspoons cumin seeds, crushed
½ teaspoon ground turmeric
900 ml (1½ pints) chicken or vegetable stock
300 ml (½ pint) milk
salt and pepper

Chilli and Stilton butter
75 g (3 oz) Stilton cheese, rind removed
50 g (2 oz) butter
½ teaspoon finely chopped fresh red chilli
2 tablespoons chopped chives (optional)

1 Preheat the slow cooker if necessary – see manufacturer's instructions. Heat the butter and oil in a large frying pan, add the onion and fry, stirring, for 5 minutes until softened but not browned.

2 Add the parsnips, apple, cumin seeds and turmeric and cook for 2 minutes. Add the stock and salt and pepper and bring to the boil. Transfer to the slow cooker pot, cover and cook on low for 4–5 hours or until the parsnips are tender.

3 Meanwhile, make the flavoured butter. Mash the cheese on a plate with the butter. Mix in the chilli and chopped chives, if using. Spoon in a line, about 10 cm (4 inches) long, on a piece of greaseproof paper or foil, cover loosely, then roll backwards and forwards to make a neat cylinder. Twist the ends of the paper or foil to seal, then chill.

4 Purée the soup in batches until smooth. Then return it to the slow cooker. Stir in the milk and cook on high for 15 minutes or until piping hot. Ladle the soup into bowls and top with thin slices of the butter and some long pieces of chive.

Gingered red lentil

This smooth, velvety but spicy soup is flavoured with ginger and cumin and topped with fried onions speckled with fennel, cumin and turmeric, lightly caramelized with a little sugar.

Serves 6
Preparation time: 30 minutes
Cooking time: 6¼–8¼ hours
Cooking temperature: low and high
Slow cooker size: standard

1 tablespoon olive oil
1 onion, chopped
2 garlic cloves, finely chopped
1 teaspoon fennel seeds, crushed
4 cm (1½ inch) fresh root ginger, peeled and
    finely chopped
900 ml (1½ pints) vegetable or chicken stock
500 g (1 lb) sweet potato, diced
150 g (5 oz) red lentils
300 ml (½ pint) full-fat milk
salt and pepper
warm naan bread, to serve

To garnish
2 tablespoons olive oil
1 onion, thinly sliced
1 teaspoon fennel seeds, crushed
½ teaspoon ground cumin
¼ teaspoon ground turmeric
1 teaspoon caster sugar

Tip
• **If you are on a dairy-free diet, add an extra 300 ml (½ pint) of stock instead of the milk at the end of step 3.**

1 Preheat the slow cooker if necessary – see manufacturer's instructions. Heat the oil in a large frying pan, add the onion and fry, stirring, for 5 minutes or until lightly browned. Add the garlic, fennel seeds and ginger and cook for 2 minutes.

2 Add the stock and salt and pepper and bring to the boil. Put the sweet potato and lentils in the slow cooker pot, pour over the hot stock mixture, cover and cook on low for 6–8 hours or until the potato and lentils are soft.

3 Purée the soup in batches and return it to the slow cooker. Stir in the milk and cook on high for 15 minutes.

4 Meanwhile, make the garnish. Heat the oil in a clean frying pan, add the onion and fry over a low heat, stirring occasionally, for 10 minutes or until softened. Stir in the spices and sugar, increase the heat slightly and fry for 5 more minutes or until golden brown.

5 Ladle the soup into bowls and sprinkle the spicy onions over the top. Serve with warm naan bread.

& sweet potato soup

Broad bean, pea & spinach soup

Serves 6

Preparation time: 30 minutes
Cooking time: 4¹/₂–5³/₄ hours
Cooking temperature: low and high
Slow cooker size: standard

1 tablespoon olive oil
1 onion, chopped
1 baking potato, about 250 g (8 oz), diced
375 g (12 oz) frozen broad beans
900 ml (1¹/₂ pints) chicken or vegetable stock
125 g (4 oz) frozen peas
100 g (3¹/₂ oz) spinach
300 ml (¹/₂ pint) full-fat milk
grated nutmeg, to taste
salt and pepper

To garnish

1 tablespoon olive oil
100 g (3¹/₂ oz) pancetta or chorizo sausage, diced
6 tablespoons double cream

1 Preheat the slow cooker if necessary – see manufacturer's instructions. Heat the oil in a large frying pan, add the onion and fry, stirring, for 5 minutes or until lightly browned. Add the potato, beans, stock and salt and pepper and bring to the boil.

2 Transfer the mixture to the slow cooker pot, cover and cook on low for 4–5 hours. Add the peas and spinach, cover and cook on high for 15–30 minutes.

3 Purée the soup in batches and return to the slow cooker. Stir in the milk, add nutmeg to taste, replace the lid and cook on high for 15 minutes or until piping hot.

4 Heat the oil in a clean frying pan and fry the pancetta or chorizo until lightly browned. Ladle the soup into bowls, swirl the cream over the top and sprinkle with the fried pancetta or chorizo.

Tip
• **Try adding 3 tablespoons of chopped mint to this soup just before serving.**

Bloody Mary soup with chilli oil

Packed with all the flavours of a chilled Bloody Mary cocktail, this smooth soup is the perfect pick-me-up or an excellent starter for a smart dinner party.

Serves 6
Preparation time: 25 minutes
Cooking time: 5–6 hours
Cooking temperature: low
Slow cooker size: standard

1 tablespoon olive oil
1 onion, chopped
1 red pepper, cored, deseeded and diced
2 celery sticks, sliced
500 g (1 lb) plum tomatoes, chopped
¼ teaspoon chilli powder
600 ml (1 pint) vegetable stock
4 teaspoons Worcestershire sauce
4 teaspoons tomato purée
2 teaspoons caster sugar
4 tablespoons vodka
salt and pepper
warm ciabatta bread, to serve

To garnish
2 tomatoes, sliced
a few celery leaves
chilli-flavoured olive oil

1 Preheat the slow cooker if necessary – see manufacturer's instructions. Heat the oil in a large frying pan, add the onion and fry, stirring, for 5 minutes or until lightly browned.

2 Stir in the red pepper, celery, tomatoes and chilli powder and cook for 2 minutes. Mix in the stock, Worcestershire sauce, tomato purée, sugar and salt and pepper and bring to the boil.

3 Transfer the mixture to the slow cooker pot, cover and cook on low for 5–6 hours. Purée it until smooth in a liquidizer or food processor, then return to the slow cooker. Stir in the vodka, cover and keep hot until required.

4 Ladle the soup into bowls and top each with a tomato slice and a small celery leaf. Drizzle chilli-flavoured oil around the tomato. Serve with warm ciabatta bread.

Crystal hot & sour chicken soup

This colourful Thai-style soup is brimming with oriental flavours. If you prefer, use the same weight of boneless, skinless chicken thighs instead of the chicken breasts.

Serves 6

Preparation time: 20 minutes
Cooking time: 5¼–7¼ hours
Cooking temperature: low and high
Slow cooker size: standard

1 tablespoon sunflower oil
1 onion, finely chopped
3 boneless, skinless chicken breasts, about
  550 g (1 lb 2 oz) in total, diced
2 garlic cloves, finely chopped
3 teaspoons red Thai curry paste
1.2 litres (2 pints) chicken stock
2 tablespoons soy sauce
1 tablespoon Thai fish sauce
125 g (4 oz) button mushrooms, sliced
1 large carrot, thinly sliced
125 g (4 oz) baby sweetcorn, sliced
50 g (2 oz) mangetout, sliced
coriander or basil leaves, torn into pieces
2 limes, cut into wedges, to serve

1 Preheat the slow cooker if necessary – see manufacturer's instructions. Heat the oil in a large frying pan, add the onion and chicken and fry, stirring, for 5 minutes or until lightly browned. Mix in the garlic and curry paste and cook for 1 minute.

2 Add the stock, soy sauce and fish sauce to the frying pan and bring to the boil. Add the mushrooms and carrot to the slow cooker pot and pour over the hot stock mixture. Cover and cook on low for 5–7 hours or until the chicken is tender.

3 Mix in the corn cobs, mangetout and herbs, cover and cook on high for 15 minutes. Ladle the soup into bowls and serve with lime wedges so that diners can squeeze over lime juice to taste.

Smoked aubergine
with anchovy toasts

Serves 6

Preparation time: 40 minutes
Cooking time: 6–8 hours
Cooking temperature: low
Slow cooker size: standard

2 large aubergines
2 tablespoons olive oil
1 large onion, chopped
2 garlic cloves, finely chopped
½ teaspoon *pimenton* (Spanish smoked paprika) or
   chilli powder
500 g (1 lb) plum tomatoes, skinned and chopped
600 ml (1 pint) vegetable or chicken stock
salt and pepper

Anchovy toasts

50 g (2 oz) can anchovy fillets, drained and finely
   chopped
75 g (3 oz) butter, softened
1 small baguette or ½ French stick, sliced into
   12 pieces

1 Preheat the slow cooker if necessary – see manufacturer's instructions. Prick each aubergine with a fork just below the stalk and cook under a preheated grill for 15 minutes, turning several times, until the skin is blistered and blackened. Transfer to a chopping board and leave to cool.

2 Heat the oil in a large frying pan, add the onion and fry, stirring, for 5 minutes.

3 Cut the aubergines in half and use a spoon to scoop the soft flesh from the skins. Roughly chop the flesh and add it to the onion with the garlic. Fry for 2 minutes, mix in the *pimentón* or chilli powder and cook for 1 minute. Stir in the tomatoes, stock and salt and pepper and bring to the boil.

4 Transfer the mixture to the slow cooker pot, cover and cook on low for 6–8 hours.

5 Purée the soup until smooth or leave chunky if preferred. Mix the anchovies with the softened butter. Toast the bread lightly and spread with the anchovy butter. Ladle the soup into bowls and float two pieces of toast on each bowl.

Dolmades

These tiny, rice-filled vine leaf parcels will evoke holiday memories of Greece. Serve as part of a mixed mezze-style starter with bowls of taramasalata, hummus and olives.

Serves 6

Preparation time: 40 minutes, plus soaking
Cooking time: 2–2½ hours
Cooking temperature: low
Slow cooker size: standard – ideally oval-shaped

100 g (3½ oz) packet vacuum-packed vine leaves
lemon wedges, to garnish
natural Greek yogurt, to serve

Filling

100 g (3½ oz) easy-cook white rice
1 small onion, finely chopped
2 garlic cloves, crushed
40 g (1½ oz) currants
25 g (1 oz) pine nuts
3 tablespoons chopped fresh mint or a pinch of dried
1 teaspoon fennel or dill seeds
2 tablespoons olive oil
finely grated rind and juice of 1 lemon
750 ml (1¼ pints) hot vegetable stock
salt and pepper

Tip

- **Vacuum-packed or canned vine leaves are available from continental delicatessen shops. If you cannot find them use halved, blanched cabbage leaves instead.**

1 Remove the vine leaves from the packet and place in a bowl of cold water. Carefully loosen the leaves and transfer to a large sinkful of cold water. Leave to soak for 30 minutes. Meanwhile, preheat the slow cooker if necessary – see manufacturer's instructions.

2 Drain the vine leaves and pat dry with kitchen paper. Spread the whole undamaged leaves out on the work surface so that the stalks are towards you and the undersides are uppermost.

3 Mix all the filling ingredients together except the lemon juice and stock. Spoon a little of the filling on to the centre of each leaf. Fold in the sides then loosely roll up each leaf to enclose the filling – if you roll the dolmades up too tightly there will be no room for the rice to expand during cooking.

4 Lay any torn or badly damaged leaves in the bottom of the slow cooker pot then arrange the vine leaf parcels in 2 or 3 layers on top. Mix the lemon juice and hot stock together and pour over the vine leaves, making sure they are covered by the liquid. Cover with the lid and cook on low for 2–2½ hours until the rice is tender.

5 Lift the dolmades out of the slow cooker, drain well and arrange on a serving plate. Serve warm or cold, garnished with lemon wedges and accompanied by spoonfuls of Greek yogurt.

Smoked salmon timbales

Serves 4

Preparation time: 30 minutes, plus chilling
Cooking time: 3–3½ hours
Cooking temperature: low
Slow cooker size: standard

200 ml (7 fl oz) full-fat crème fraîche
4 egg yolks
grated rind and juice of ½ lemon
1 small growing pot of basil
200 g (7 oz) sliced smoked salmon
salt and pepper
lemon wedges, to garnish (optional)

1 Preheat the slow cooker if necessary – see manufacturer's instructions. Lightly butter 4 individual 150 ml (¼ pint) metal moulds and line their bases with circles of nonstick baking or greaseproof paper.

2 Put the crème fraîche in a bowl and gradually beat in the egg yolks then the lemon rind and juice and season with salt and pepper. Chop half the basil and 75 g (3 oz) smoked salmon then stir both into the crème fraîche mixture.

3 Pour the mixture into the prepared moulds then stand the moulds in the slow cooker pot – there is no need to cover them with foil. Pour hot water around the moulds to come halfway up their sides then add the cooker lid and cook on low for 3–3½ hours or until the moulds are set.

4 Carefully remove the moulds from the slow cooker using a tea towel and leave to cool at room temperature. Transfer to the refrigerator and chill for at least 4 hours or overnight.

5 To serve, arrange the remaining smoked salmon on 4 serving plates. Loosen the edges of the timbales with a knife dipped in hot water then invert on to the serving plates and remove the moulds. Smooth any rough areas with the side of the knife and remove the paper lining discs. Garnish with the remaining smoked salmon and basil leaves. Serve with lemon wedges, if using.

Brandied duck,

Serves 6

Preparation time: 45 minutes, plus overnight chilling
Cooking time: 5–6 hours
Cooking temperature: high
Slow cooker size: standard

175 g (6 oz) rindless, smoked streaky bacon
1 tablespoon olive oil
1 onion, chopped
2 boneless spare rib pork chops, about 275 g (9 oz)
2 boneless duck breasts, about 375 g (12 oz),
  fat removed
2 garlic cloves, chopped
3 tablespoons brandy
75 g (3 oz) fresh breadcrumbs
50 g (2 oz) sun-dried tomatoes in oil, drained
  and chopped
3 pickled walnuts, drained and roughly chopped
1 egg, beaten
1 tablespoon green peppercorns, roughly crushed
salt

Tip
• **Black olives or prunes could be used in place
  of the pickled walnuts.**

walnut & green peppercorn terrine

Take this impressive pâté on a summer picnic or serve it at an alfresco weekend lunch with a bottle of red wine. It tastes lovely sliced and served with French bread, tomatoes drizzled with olive oil and garlicky marinated olives.

1 Preheat the slow cooker if necessary – see manufacturer's instructions. Lay the bacon rashers on a chopping board and stretch each one, using the flat of a large cook's knife, until half as long again. Drape the rashers across the inside of a 15 cm (6 inch) diameter, deep heatproof soufflé dish that will fit comfortably in your slow cooker pot. Press the bacon up the sides of the dish so it is covered and leave the ends overhanging the dish.

2 Heat the oil in a frying pan, add the onion and fry, stirring, for 5 minutes until softened. Finely chop or mince the pork and 1 of the duck breasts. Cut the second duck breast into long thin slices. Stir the garlic, minced or chopped pork and duck into the frying pan and cook for 3 minutes. Add the brandy, flame with a match and stand well back.

3 When the flames have subsided, stir in the breadcrumbs, sun-dried tomatoes, walnuts, beaten egg, peppercorns and a little salt. Mix well then spoon half the mixture into the bacon-lined dish and press down firmly. Top with the sliced duck then the remaining pork and walnut mixture. Fold the bacon ends over the top of the mixture, adding any leftover rashers to cover the gaps. Cover with foil.

4 Place an upturned saucer in the base of the slow cooker pot, add foil straps or a string pudding bowl lifter (see page 15) then the soufflé dish. Pour boiling water around the dish to come halfway up its sides. Cover the cooker with the lid and cook on high for 5–6 hours or until the meat juices run clear when the centre of the terrine is pierced with a knife.

5 Carefully lift the terrine out of the slow cooker using the foil straps or string pudding bowl lifter and oven gloves. Stand the dish on a plate, remove the foil top and replace with greaseproof paper. Weight down the top of the terrine with measuring weights or unopened cans of food resting on top of a small plate. Transfer to the refrigerator when cool enough and chill overnight until firm.

6 Remove the weights and greaseproof paper from the terrine. Run a knife around the inside edge of the dish to loosen the terrine, then invert the dish on to a chopping board or serving plate. Jerk to release, then lift the dish off the terrine. Cut into thick slices and serve.

Meat, poultry & game

Malaysian beef & aubergine curry

Quick and easy to put together, this spicy curry tastes delicious topped with pak choi which has been stir-fried with a little ginger, and accompanied by plain rice.

Serves 4

Preparation time: 25 minutes
Cooking time: 8–9 hours
Cooking temperature: low
Slow cooker size: standard

1 large onion
3–4 garlic cloves
2 tablespoons sunflower oil
500 g (1 lb) braising beef, diced
1 large aubergine, cut into chunks
2 tablespoons red Thai curry paste
1 tablespoon fish sauce
400 ml (14 fl oz) can coconut milk
boiled rice, to serve

1 Preheat the slow cooker if necessary – see manufacturer's instructions. Process or very finely chop the onion and garlic until almost paste-like. Heat the oil in a frying pan, add the onion and garlic and fry, stirring, for 2—3 minutes until softened.

2 Add the beef and aubergine, a few pieces at a time, and fry until browned. Stir in the curry paste, fish sauce and coconut milk. Bring to the boil then transfer to the slow cooker pot.

3 Cover with the lid and cook on low for 8–9 hours until the meat is tender. Serve with plain boiled rice and stir-fried pak choi, if liked.

Tip
- **If you prefer to use creamed coconut rather than canned coconut milk, cook the beef in 400 ml (14 fl oz) chicken stock and crumble in 50 g (2 oz) creamed coconut at the end of cooking.**

Beef & ale hotpot

This full-bodied traditional hotpot topped with thinly sliced potatoes also has a surprise layer of sliced celeriac, which adds a delicious and subtle celery flavour to this dish. Baby carrots make an ideal accompaniment.

Serves 6

Preparation time: 30 minutes
Cooking time: 5–6 hours
Cooking temperature: high
Slow cooker size: large or extra large

2 tablespoons sunflower oil
1 kg (2 lb) braising beef, trimmed of fat and cubed
1 large onion, chopped
3 tablespoons plain flour
500 ml (17 fl oz) can brown ale, stout or barley wine
4 teaspoons wholegrain mustard
3 teaspoons soft light or dark brown sugar
2 tablespoons tomato purée
450 ml (¾ pint) hot beef stock
425 g (14 oz) celeriac, peeled and thinly sliced
625 g (1¼ lb) similarly sized baking potatoes, peeled and thinly sliced
25 g (1 oz) butter, melted
salt and pepper
finely chopped chives, to garnish (optional)

1 Preheat the slow cooker if necessary – see manufacturer's instructions. Heat 1 tablespoon of the oil in a large frying pan, gradually add half the beef and fry over a high heat, stirring until browned. Remove the beef from the pan with a slotted spoon and transfer to a plate.

2 Heat the remaining oil in the pan, add the remaining beef and the onion and fry over a high heat, stirring until browned. Stir in the flour, then add the beer, mustard, sugar, tomato purée and plenty of salt and pepper. Bring to the boil, stirring, then transfer to the slow cooker pot with the fried beef. Stir in the hot stock.

3 Arrange the celeriac slices overlapping each other on top of the beef then cover with the sliced potatoes. Brush with the melted butter, sprinkle with a little extra salt and pepper then cover the cooker with the lid and cook on high for 5–6 hours. Garnish with a sprinkling of finely chopped chives, if using, to finish.

Tips
- **To make in a smaller slow cooker, halve the ingredient quantities and cook for the same length of time.**
- **If the slow cooker pot fits under your grill, you may like to brown the top of the potatoes before serving.**

pudding

Serves 4

Preparation time: 40 minutes
Cooking time: 5–6 hours
Cooking temperature: high
Slow cooker size: standard

25 g (1 oz) butter, plus extra for greasing
1 tablespoon sunflower oil
2 large onions, roughly chopped
2 teaspoons caster sugar
100 g (3½ oz) cup mushrooms, sliced
1 tablespoon plain or self-raising flour
150 ml (¼ pint) hot beef stock
1 teaspoon Dijon mustard
1 tablespoon Worcestershire sauce
700 g (1 lb 6 oz) rump steak,
   trimmed of fat and thinly sliced
salt and pepper

Pastry
300 g (10 oz) self-raising flour
½ teaspoon salt
150 g (5 oz) shredded suet
200 ml (7 fl oz) water

1 Preheat the slow cooker if necessary – see manufacturer's instructions. Heat the butter and oil in a frying pan, add the onions and fry for 5 minutes until softened. Sprinkle the sugar over the onions and fry for 5 more minutes until browned. Add the mushrooms and fry for 2–3 minutes, then stir in the flour.

2 Mix together the stock, mustard, Worcestershire sauce and salt and pepper in a jug.

3 To make the pastry, put the flour, salt and suet in a bowl and mix well. Gradually stir in the water to make a soft but not sticky dough. Knead the dough lightly then roll out on a floured surface to a circle 33 cm (13 inches) in diameter. Cut a quarter segment out of the circle and reserve for the lid.

4 Butter a 1.5 litre (2½ pint) pudding basin that will fit comfortably in your slow cooker pot with a space of at least 1.5 cm (¾ inch) all the way around. Lift the remaining pastry into the basin. Bring the cut edges together, overlapping them slightly so that the basin is completely lined with pastry, and press them together to seal.

5 Fill the pastry-lined pudding basin with alternate layers of fried onion and mushrooms and sliced steak. Pour the hot stock mixture over the top. Pat the reserved piece of pastry into a round the same size as the top of the basin. Fold the top edges of the pastry in the basin over the meat filling, brush with a little water then cover with the pastry lid.

6 Cover with a large circle of buttered and pleated foil and dome the foil 'lid' slightly so that there is room for the pastry to rise. Tie the foil in place with a length of string tied around the basin, under the rim, and add a string handle (see page 15). Stand the basin in the slow cooker pot on top of an upturned saucer. Pour boiling water into the slow cooker pot to come halfway up the sides of the pudding basin.

7 Add the lid and cook the pudding on high for 5–6 hours. Remove the basin from the slow cooker then remove the string and foil – the pastry should have risen and feel dry to the touch. Serve.

Burgundy beef stew

This homely stew topped with light and fluffy horseradish-flavoured, chive-speckled dumplings is just the thing to restore flagging spirits after a long hectic day, and requires no accompaniments. Simply spoon into shallow dishes and enjoy.

Serves 4

Preparation time: 35 minutes
Cooking time: 8–10½ hours
Cooking temperature: low and high
Slow cooker size: standard

2 tablespoons olive oil
750 g (1½ lb) braising beef, trimmed of fat and cubed
1 large onion, chopped
2–3 garlic cloves, chopped
2 tablespoons plain flour
300 ml (½ pint) Burgundy red wine
300 ml (½ pint) beef stock
1 tablespoon tomato purée
2 bay leaves
150 g (5 oz) baby carrots, larger ones halved
250 g (8 oz) leeks, trimmed, cleaned and thinly sliced
salt and pepper

Horseradish dumplings

150 g (5 oz) self-raising flour
75 g (3 oz) shredded suet
2 teaspoons creamed horseradish
3 tablespoons chopped chives
5–7 tablespoons water
salt and pepper

1 Preheat the slow cooker if necessary – see manufacturer's instructions. Heat the oil in a frying pan, add the beef, a few cubes at a time, until all the pieces have been added to the pan. Fry over a high heat until just beginning to brown then add the onion and fry, stirring, for 5 minutes.

2 Stir in the garlic and flour then gradually mix in the wine and stock. Add the tomato purée and bay leaves and season with salt and pepper. Bring to the boil then transfer the mixture to the slow cooker pot. Cover with the lid and cook on low for 7–9 hours.

3 Stir the stew then add the carrots and cook on high for 30–45 minutes. Meanwhile, make the dumplings: mix the flour, suet, horseradish, chives and salt and pepper in a bowl. Stir in enough water to make a soft but not sticky dough. With floured hands, shape into 8 balls.

4 Stir the leeks into the stew then add the dumplings, replace the lid and cook for another 30–45 minutes until the dumplings are light and fluffy. Spoon into shallow dishes and serve, remembering to remove the bay leaves.

with horseradish dumplings

Braised oxtail with port

Serves 4

Preparation time: 25 minutes
Cooking time: 9–10 hours
Cooking temperature: low
Slow cooker size: standard

1 tablespoon sunflower oil, plus extra for brushing
1 well-trimmed oxtail, about 1 kg (2 lb),
   thickly sliced
1 large onion, chopped
2 tablespoons plain flour
250 ml (8 fl oz) ruby port
450 ml (¾ pint) beef stock
1 cinnamon stick, halved
1 teaspoon ground mace
2 teaspoons juniper berries, roughly crushed
2 tablespoons tomato purée
1 red pepper, halved and cored
salt and pepper

1 Preheat the slow cooker if necessary – see manufacturer's instructions. Heat the oil in a frying pan, add the oxtail and fry, in batches if necessary, until browned. Lift out and place on a plate.

2 Add the onion to the pan and fry until pale golden. Stir in the flour then add the port, stock, cinnamon, mace, juniper berries, tomato purée and season with salt and pepper. Bring to the boil, stirring.

3 Transfer the oxtail to the slow cooker pot then pour in the hot stock mixture, making sure that the oxtail is completely covered. Add the lid and cook on low for 9–10 hours. Just before serving, put the red pepper halves, skin side uppermost, on a piece of foil in a grill pan. Brush with oil and grill until the skin is blackened. Cool for 10 minutes then peel off the skin and cut the pepper into thin slices.

4 Spoon the oxtail and sauce into shallow dishes, discarding the cinnamon stick. Garnish with the grilled sliced red pepper and serve with cannellini bean mash. Provide a separate bowl for the bones or remove them before serving – the meat is so tender after such long cooking, it almost falls off the bone.

Mince & macaroni

This is a good midweek supper standby, based on minced beef or lamb, a can of tomatoes and dried macaroni. You can replace 150 ml (¼ pint) of the stock with red wine if liked.

Serves 4

Preparation time: 20 minutes
Cooking time: 8–9 hours
Cooking temperature: low
Slow cooker size: standard

15 g (½ oz) mixed dried mushrooms
150 ml (¼ pint) boiling water
1 tablespoon olive oil
500 g (1 lb) minced beef or lamb
1 large onion, chopped
2 garlic cloves, chopped
400 g (13 oz) can chopped tomatoes
450 ml (¾ pint) chicken stock
2 tablespoons tomato purée
¼ teaspoon grated nutmeg
small bunch of rosemary
250 g (8 oz) macaroni
3 tablespoons pine nuts, toasted
salt and pepper

1 Preheat the slow cooker if necessary – see manufacturer's instructions. Put the mushrooms in a bowl, pour over the boiling water and leave to soak for 20 minutes.

2 Meanwhile, heat the oil in a frying pan. Add the minced meat and onion and fry, stirring, for 5 minutes until browned. Add the garlic then stir in the canned tomatoes, stock, tomato purée and nutmeg. Tear the leaves off 3 of the rosemary sprigs and add to the mince with the reconstituted dried mushrooms and their soaking liquid, and salt and pepper.

3 Transfer the mixture to the slow cooker pot, cover with the lid and cook on low for 8–9 hours. When ready to serve, cook the macaroni in a saucepan of boiling water until tender. Drain and mix into the cooked mince. Spoon on to individual plates and top with the toasted pine nuts and rosemary leaves, stripped from the remaining sprigs.

Tip
• **To make in a larger slow cooker, increase the ingredient quantities by half as much again and cook for the same length of time.**

Bobotie

This spiced meatloaf is a South African dish, which can be eaten hot with spiced rice or cold with tomato salad.

Serves 4–5

Preparation time: 30 minutes
Cooking time: 5¹/₂–6¹/₂ hours
Cooking temperature: high
Slow cooker size: standard

1 tablespoon sunflower oil
500 g (1 lb) lean minced beef
1 onion, finely chopped
2 garlic cloves, finely chopped
4 teaspoons curry paste
1 tablespoon red or white wine vinegar
1 tablespoon tomato purée
50 g (2 oz) sultanas
1 banana, chopped
50 g (2 oz) fresh white breadcrumbs
3 small bay leaves
salt and pepper

Topping
2 eggs
large pinch ground turmeric
4 tablespoons milk

1 Preheat the slow cooker if necessary – see manufacturer's instructions. Heat the oil in a large frying pan, add the mince and onion and fry over a high heat, stirring, until the mince is evenly browned.

2 Add the garlic, curry paste, vinegar and tomato purée, then the sultanas, chopped banana and breadcrumbs to the pan and season with salt and pepper.

3 Spoon the mixture into a lightly oiled soufflé dish or ovenproof dish, 13 cm (5 inches) across and 9 cm (3 inches) high, and press it into an even layer. Press the bay leaves on top and cover with foil.

4 Use foil straps or a string handle to lower the dish into the slow cooker pot (see page 15). Pour boiling water into the pot so that it comes halfway up the sides of the dish. Cover and cook on high for 5–6 hours or until the meatloaf is cooked all the way through.

5 Make the topping. Beat together the eggs, turmeric, milk and salt and pepper and pour the mixture over the bay leaves. Cover loosely with foil and cook on high for 30 minutes or until set. Carefully lift the dish out of the slow cooker pot and serve warm or cold.

Thi bo kho

This Vietnamese beef stew is flavoured with yellow bean paste and five spice powder. Serve it with rice or fried noodles for a tasty midweek supper.

Serves 4

Preparation time: 30 minutes
Cooking time: 8–10 hours
Cooking temperature: low
Slow cooker size: standard

1 tablespoon sunflower oil
250 g (8 oz) shallots, halved
750 g (1½ lb) braising beef, cubed
2 garlic cloves, finely chopped
2 tablespoons plain flour
450 ml (¾ pint) beef stock
3 tablespoons yellow bean paste
grated rind of 1 lemon, plus extra rind to garnish
1 teaspoon five spice powder
salt and pepper
100 g (3½ oz) well-rinsed bean sprouts, to garnish
rice or fried noodles, to serve

1 Preheat the slow cooker if necessary – see manufacturer's instructions. Heat the oil in a large frying pan, add the shallots and fry for 5 minutes or until golden. Remove them from the pan with a slotted spoon and transfer to a plate.

2 Add the beef to the pan, a few pieces at a time, until all the meat has been added, then cook over a high heat, stirring until evenly browned. Add the garlic and cook for 2 minutes.

3 Stir in the flour, then gradually mix in the stock. Add the yellow bean paste, lemon rind and five spice powder and season with salt and pepper. Bring to the boil, stirring.

4 Spoon the beef mixture into the slow cooker pot, add the shallots and press the meat below the surface of the liquid. Cover and cook on low for 8–10 hours or until the meat is tender.

5 Garnish the casserole with stir-fried bean sprouts and extra lemon rind and serve with rice or fried noodles.

Tip
• If you use stock cubes, choose one with a mild flavour so that it does not overpower the yellow bean paste.

Olive & lemon meatballs

Buying a pack of mince in the weekly supermarket dash needn't mean Spaghetti Bolognese again. Here the mince is flavoured with black olives and lemon rind, shaped into meatballs and gently simmered with a rich tomato sauce.

Serves 4

Preparation time: 30 minutes
Cooking time: 6–8 hours
Cooking temperature: low
Slow cooker size: standard

Meatballs
50 g (2 oz) pitted black olives, chopped
grated rind of ½ lemon
500 g (1 lb) extra lean minced beef
1 egg yolk
salt and pepper

Sauce
1 tablespoon olive oil
1 onion, chopped
2 garlic cloves, finely chopped
400 g (13 oz) can chopped tomatoes
1 teaspoon caster sugar
150 ml (¼ pint) chicken stock

To garnish
grated rind of 1 lemon
small basil leaves

1 Preheat the slow cooker if necessary – see manufacturer's instructions. Make the meatballs. Put all the ingredients in a bowl and mix with a wooden spoon. Wet your hands and shape the mixture into 20 balls.

2 Heat the oil in a large frying pan, add the meatballs and cook over a high heat, turning until browned on all sides. Lift them out of pan with a slotted spoon and transfer to a plate.

3 Make the sauce. Add the onion to the pan and fry, stirring, for 5 minutes or until lightly browned. Add the garlic, tomatoes, sugar, stock and salt and pepper and bring to the boil, stirring.

4 Transfer the meatballs to the slow cooker pot, pour over the hot sauce, cover and cook on low for 6–8 hours. Sprinkle with lemon rind and basil leaves to garnish. Serve with tagliatelle tossed with chopped basil and melted butter.

with tomato sauce

with bay

Bay leaves have been popular in meaty stews since Roman times, and here they are combined with root ginger for a rustic-style casserole that is delicious served with mashed potato or celeriac.

Serves 4

Preparation time: 20 minutes
Cooking time: 8–10 hours
Cooking temperature: low
Slow cooker size: standard

2 tablespoons olive oil
750 g (1½ lb) lean braising beef, cubed
1 onion, chopped
2 tablespoons plain flour
450 ml (¾ pint) beef stock
1 tablespoon tomato purée
1 tablespoon balsamic vinegar
2 teaspoons dark muscovado sugar
3 bay leaves
4 cm (1½ inch) fresh root ginger, peeled
   and finely chopped
salt and pepper
baby carrots, to serve

1 Preheat the slow cooker if necessary – see manufacturer's instructions. Heat the oil in a large frying pan, add the beef, a few pieces at a time, until all the meat has been added, then fry over a high heat, stirring, until evenly browned. Lift out of the pan with a slotted spoon and transfer to a plate.

2 Add the onion to the pan and fry, stirring, for 5 minutes or until softened and lightly browned. Stir in the flour, then mix in the stock, tomato purée, vinegar, sugar, bay leaves and ginger. Season with salt and pepper and bring to the boil.

3 Transfer the beef to the slow cooker pot, pour over the hot stock, cover and cook on low for 8–10 hours. Serve with steamed baby carrots tossed with a little butter.

Tip
- **This casserole would also be delicious with horseradish dumplings (see page 62). Shape and add the dumplings 30–45 minutes before the end of cooking and increase the temperature from low to high.**

Beef adobo

This beef recipe, which is flavoured with soy sauce and wine vinegar, is traditionally eaten in the Philippines, but it's also a popular dish in Spain and Gibraltar.

Serves 4

Preparation time: 25 minutes
Cooking time: 8–10 hours
Cooking temperature: low
Slow cooker size: standard

1 tablespoon sunflower oil
750 g (1½ lb) braising beef, trimmed of fat and cubed
1 large onion, sliced
2 garlic cloves, finely chopped
2 tablespoons plain flour
450 ml (¾ pint) beef stock
4 tablespoons soy sauce
4 tablespoons rice or wine vinegar
1 tablespoon caster sugar
2 bay leaves
juice of 1 lime
salt and pepper
rice, to serve

To garnish
1 carrot, cut into thin sticks
½ bunch of spring onions, cut into shreds
coriander leaves

1 Preheat the slow cooker if necessary – see manufacturer's instructions. Heat the oil in a large frying pan and add the beef, a few pieces at a time, until all the meat has been added. Fry over a high heat, turning until evenly browned, lift out of the pan with a slotted spoon and transfer to a plate.

2 Add the onion to the pan and fry for 5 minutes or until it is just beginning to brown. Mix in the garlic and cook for 2 minutes. Stir in the flour, then gradually mix in the stock. Add the soy sauce, vinegar, sugar, bay leaves and salt and pepper and bring to the boil, stirring.

3 Transfer the beef to the slow cooker pot, pour over the onion and stock mixture, cover and cook on low for 8–10 hours.

4 Stir in lime juice to taste. Serve in shallow bowls lined with rice and garnish with carrot sticks, shredded spring onion and coriander leaves.

Spiced lamb tagine

Don't be put off by the long list of ingredients for this recipe. This mellow Moroccan-inspired mince dish is quick and easy to cook and makes just 500 g (1 lb) mince go a long way.

Serves 6–8

Preparation time: 35 minutes
Cooking time: 8½–10½ hours
Cooking temperature: low
Slow cooker size: large or extra large

1 tablespoon olive oil
500 g (1 lb) minced lamb
1 large onion, chopped
2–3 garlic cloves, chopped
3.5 cm (1½ inch) piece of root ginger, peeled
   and finely chopped
1 teaspoon turmeric
1 teaspoon ground cinnamon
½ teaspoon ground allspice
2 tablespoons plain flour
400 g (13 oz) can chopped tomatoes
750 ml (1¼ pints) lamb or chicken stock
1 tablespoon tomato purée
300 g (10 oz) new potatoes, scrubbed and halved
   or quartered depending on size
300 g (10 oz) butternut squash, deseeded, peeled
   and diced
2 carrots, diced
50 g (2 oz) raisins
300 g (10 oz) frozen broad beans
150 g (5 oz) frozen peas
small bunch of mint
salt and pepper
couscous, to serve

1 Preheat the slow cooker if necessary – see manufacturer's instructions. Heat the oil in a large frying pan. Add the mince and onion and fry, stirring, for 5 minutes until the mince is browned. Stir in the garlic, root ginger, spices and flour, then add the canned tomatoes, stock and tomato purée.

2 Mix in the potatoes, butternut squash, carrots and raisins then season with salt and pepper. Bring to the boil then transfer to the slow cooker pot. Cover with the lid and cook on low for 8–10 hours.

3 Stir the tagine then sprinkle the frozen vegetables over the top. Replace the lid and cook for another 20–30 minutes until the vegetables are hot. Spoon on to individual plates, sprinkle with torn mint leaves and serve with couscous.

Greek–style lamb shanks

Long slow cooking brings out the natural sweetness of the lamb, which is complemented by the delicate lemon flavour of the crushed coriander seeds and bay leaves. Sliced lamb shoulder or leg steaks can also be cooked in this way if shanks are unavailable.

Serves 4

Preparation time: 20 minutes
Cooking time: 5–7 hours
Cooking temperature: high
Slow cooker size: standard

1 tablespoon olive oil
4 lamb shanks, about 1.5 kg (3 lb)
1 large onion, thinly sliced
4 teaspoons coriander seeds, roughly crushed
2 tablespoons plain flour
600 ml (1 pint) chicken or lamb stock
150 ml (1/4 pint) dry sherry, dry cider or white wine
4 bay leaves
2 teaspoons honey
salt and pepper
mashed potato or rice and a green salad, to serve

To garnish
oregano leaves
grated lemon rind

Tips

- **If your slow cooker has a maximum working capacity of less than 2.5 litres (4 pints) then cook only 3 lamb shanks, using the same quantity of the other ingredients.**

- **To make in an extra large slow cooker, with a maximum working capacity of 4.5 litres (8 pints), increase the ingredient quantities by half as much again.**

1 Preheat the slow cooker if necessary – see manufacturer's instructions. Heat the oil in a frying pan, add the lamb shanks and brown on all sides. Transfer them to the slow cooker pot, arranging them so that they almost stand up with the thickest parts on the bottom of the pot.

2 Add the onion to the frying pan and fry, stirring, for 5 minutes until lightly browned. Add the coriander seeds and cook for 1 minute. Stir in the flour then add the stock, sherry, cider or wine, bay leaves and honey and season with salt and pepper. Bring to the boil then pour over the lamb. Cover with the lid and cook on high for 5–7 hours until the meat almost falls off the bone. (The high setting is necessary because the shanks are much denser than cubed meat.) Turn the meat once during cooking, if possible.

3 Transfer the lamb shanks to a serving bowl, cover and keep hot. Carefully lift the slow cooker pot out of the base unit using oven gloves, pour the contents into a saucepan and boil rapidly to reduce the liquid by half. (Alternatively, simply thicken the liquid with a little cornflour mixed to a smooth paste with cold water instead.) Spoon the sauce and onions over the lamb, discarding the bay leaves, then garnish with oregano leaves and lemon rind. Serve with creamy mashed potato, or with rice and a green salad mixed with black olives.

This classic French-style lamb stew, which is slowly cooked with red wine and finished with shallots and bacon, is particularly delicious served with mashed celeriac or potatoes and green beans. The prunes add a marvellous flavour to the gravy.

Serves 4

Preparation time: 30 minutes
Cooking time: 7½–8½ hours
Cooking temperature: low
Slow cooker size: standard

2 tablespoons olive oil
700 g (1 lb 6 oz) lean lamb, diced
1 large onion, chopped
50 g (2 oz) streaky bacon, rinded and diced
2 garlic cloves, chopped
1 tablespoon plain flour
200 ml (7 fl oz) red wine
300 ml (½ pint) lamb or chicken stock
1 tablespoon tomato purée
75 g (3 oz) pitted prunes (optional)
fresh or dried bouquet garni
salt and pepper

To finish

15 g (½ oz) butter
1 tablespoon olive oil
175 g (6 oz) shallots, halved if large
50 g (2 oz) streaky bacon, rinded and diced

1 Preheat the slow cooker if necessary – see manufacturer's instructions. Heat the oil in a frying pan then add the lamb, a few pieces at a time, until it has all been added to the pan. Cook over a high heat until browned. Drain and transfer to a plate.

2 Add the onion and bacon to the pan and fry for 5 minutes until pale golden. Add the garlic, then stir in the flour. Add the wine, stock, tomato purée, prunes, if using, and bouquet garni and season with salt and pepper. Bring to the boil, stirring.

3 Transfer the onion mixture to the slow cooker pot, add the lamb and mix together. Cover with the lid and cook on low for 7–8 hours. To finish, heat the butter and oil in the cleaned frying pan, add the shallots and bacon and fry until golden. Stir into the lamb casserole and cook for 30 minutes then serve.

Tips

- **To make in a larger slow cooker, increase the ingredient quantities by half as much again and cook for the same length of time.**

- **Use braising beef in place of the lamb if preferred.**

77

Abruzzi lamb

The foothills of the Abruzzi, a mountainous region in central Italy, are famous for lamb dishes, especially those slowly cooked with garlic, olive oil and tomatoes.

Serves 4–5
Preparation time: 30 minutes
Cooking time: 8–10 hours
Cooking temperature: low
Slow cooker size: standard

1 tablespoon olive oil
750 g (1½ lb) lean lamb, leg or chump steaks, cubed
75 g (3 oz) pancetta, diced
1 large onion, chopped
2 garlic cloves, finely chopped
2 tablespoons plain flour
300 ml (½ pint) lamb or chicken stock
1 tablespoon tomato purée
2 teaspoons light muscovado sugar
2–3 sprigs of rosemary
250 g (8 oz) cherry tomatoes
salt and pepper

To serve
rigatoni or pappardelle
green salad

1 Preheat the slow cooker if necessary – see manufacturer's instructions. Heat the oil in a large frying pan and add the lamb, a few pieces at a time, until all the meat has been added. Fry over a high heat, stirring until evenly browned, then lift the lamb out of the pan with a slotted spoon and transfer to a plate.

2 Add the pancetta and onion to the pan and fry, stirring, for 5 minutes or until lightly browned. Add the garlic and cook for 2 minutes. Stir in the flour, then mix in the stock. Add the tomato purée, sugar, rosemary and salt and pepper and bring to the boil, stirring.

3 Spoon the meat and any juices into the slow cooker pot, pour the hot onion mixture over the top, then add the whole tomatoes. Cover with the lid, then cook on low for 8–10 hours or until the lamb is tender.

4 Serve the lamb spooned over cooked pasta such as pappardelle or rigatoni and accompanied with a salad.

Tips
- If you like, replace 150 ml (¼ pint) stock with the same quantity of red wine.
- If you do not have any fresh rosemary, use a small amount of dried rosemary.

Lamb, port &

This classic and flavour-filled hotpot is cooked with ruby port and dried cranberries. A slow cooker will not brown the potatoes, but if you like them a little crispy you can pop the pot under the grill for a few minutes before serving.

Serves 4

Preparation time: 35 minutes
Cooking time: 7–8 hours
Cooking temperature: high
Slow cooker size: standard

1 tablespoon sunflower oil
6 lamb chump chops, about 750 g (1½ lb), halved
1 onion, chopped
125 g (4 oz) button mushrooms, sliced
2 tablespoons plain flour
450 ml (¾ pint) lamb stock
125 ml (4 fl oz) ruby port
1 tablespoon tomato purée
1 tablespoon cranberry sauce
25 g (1 oz) dried cranberries (optional)
700 g (1 lb 7 oz) baking potatoes, thinly sliced
salt and pepper
chopped parsley, to garnish (optional)

1 Preheat the slow cooker if necessary – see manufacturer's instructions. Heat the oil in a large frying pan, add the lamb and fry over a high heat until browned on both sides. Lift out with a slotted spoon and transfer to a plate.

2 Add the onion to the pan and fry, stirring, for 5 minutes or until lightly browned. Add the mushrooms and cook for 2 minutes. Stir in the flour, then gradually mix in the stock and port. Add the tomato purée, cranberry sauce and dried cranberries, if using, and season to taste with salt and pepper. Bring to the boil, stirring.

3 Put the pieces of lamb in the base of the slow cooker pot, pour over the hot sauce and arrange the sliced potatoes on top, overlapping the slices in two layers. Gently press the potatoes down into the sauce, cover and cook on high for 7–8 hours or until the lamb and potatoes are tender. Sprinkle with parsley, if liked, and spoon into bowls.

Tip

• If you have an oven with a grill element you might like to brown the top of the potatoes before serving. Dot them with a little butter and transfer the slow cooker pot to the oven under a preheated grill for 4–5 minutes.

cranberry hotpot

Kleftico-style lamb

This moist half shoulder of lamb is flavoured with wine, lemon and honey and is so tender that it practically falls off the bone as you serve it. Serve with plain boiled potatoes or rice mixed with chopped parsley and toasted pine nuts.

Serves 4

Preparation time: 25 minutes
Cooking time: 7–8 hours
Cooking temperature: high
Slow cooker size: standard oval

½ shoulder of lamb, 900 g–1 kg (1 lb 14 oz–2 lb)
2 garlic cloves, sliced
1 tablespoon olive oil
2 large onions, halved and thinly sliced
2 tablespoons plain flour
300 ml (½ pint) lamb stock
150 ml (¼ pint) white wine or extra stock
½ lemon, thinly sliced
1 tablespoon honey
4–5 sprigs of rosemary, plus extra to garnish
50 g (2 oz) stoned dates, halved
40 g (1½ oz) raisins
salt and pepper

1 Preheat the slow cooker if necessary – see manufacturer's instructions. Make small slits at intervals over the top of the lamb down through the fat and into the meat and insert a small slice of garlic into each slit.

2 Heat the oil in a large frying pan and fry the lamb over a high heat until browned all over. Lift the lamb out of the pan and transfer it to a plate. Add the onions and fry, stirring, for 5 minutes or until lightly browned. Stir in the flour, then mix in the stock, wine, if using, lemon slices and honey. Season with salt and pepper and bring to the boil.

3 Put 2 rosemary sprigs in the base of the slow cooker, add the lamb, the remaining rosemary, the dates and raisins, then pour over the hot stock mixture. Cover and cook on high for 7–8 hours. Serve in shallow bowls, garnished with rosemary.

Tips
- **This recipe is best suited to an oval slow cooker. Check that the lamb will fit in your slow cooker before you begin.**
- **The lamb will simply fall off the bone when it's cooked, so don't try to carve it into neat slices.**

Spiced pork chops with sweet potato

A sweet and sour mix of cubed sweet potato, diced cooking apple and pork chops, gently simmered with an aromatic blend of allspice, cinnamon and chilli.

Serves 4

Preparation time: 30 minutes
Cooking time: 7–8 hours
Cooking temperature: high
Slow cooker size: standard

1 tablespoon olive oil
4 pork shoulder steaks or boneless spare rib chops, about 700 g (1 lb 7 oz)
1 onion, chopped
2 garlic cloves, finely chopped
2 tablespoons plain flour
450 ml (¾ pint) chicken stock
400 g (13 oz) can chopped tomatoes
½ teaspoon ground allspice
½ teaspoon ground cinnamon
1 large dried chilli (optional)
1 cooking apple, about 250 g (8 oz), cored, peeled and diced
2 large sweet potatoes, about 700 g (1 lb 7 oz), cut into 2.5 cm (1 inch) cubes
salt and pepper

1 Preheat the slow cooker if necessary – see manufacturer's instructions. Heat the oil in a large frying pan, add the pork and fry over a high heat until browned on both sides. Lift it out with a slotted spoon and transfer to a plate.

2 Add the onion to the pan and fry, stirring, for 5 minutes or until lightly browned. Mix in the garlic, then the flour. Gradually stir in the stock and tomatoes, then the spices and chilli, if using, and season to taste with salt and pepper. Bring to the boil.

3 Put the pork in the slow cooker pot, add the apple and sweet potatoes and pour over the sauce. Cover and cook on high for 7–8 hours. Spoon into bowls and serve with warmed bread.

Tip
• Although there may seem to be a lot of sauce at the end, it is vital so that the potatoes cook evenly. Serve with spoons and lots of bread to mop it up.

Peppered pork pot

This Italian-inspired casserole is delicious served with mashed potatoes or creamy soft polenta.

Serves 4

Preparation time: 25 minutes
Cooking time: 8–10 hours
Cooking temperature: low
Slow cooker size: standard

1 tablespoon olive oil
4 boneless spare rib pork chops, about 700 g (1 lb 6 oz)
1 onion, chopped
1 red pepper, cored, deseeded and sliced
1 orange or yellow pepper, cored, deseeded and sliced
2 garlic cloves, chopped
2 tablespoons plain flour
400 g (13 oz) can chopped tomatoes
200 ml (7 fl oz) chicken stock
a few thyme sprigs
salt and pepper
mashed potatoes or polenta, to serve

1 Preheat the slow cooker if necessary – see manufacturer's instructions. Heat the oil in a frying pan, add the pork chops and brown on both sides. Remove and transfer to a plate.

2 Add the onion to the pan and fry, stirring, for 5 minutes until lightly browned. Stir in the peppers and garlic and fry for 1 minute. Stir in the flour, then add the canned tomatoes, stock and thyme and season with salt and pepper. Bring to the boil, stirring.

3 Transfer the pork chops to the slow cooker pot and cover with the tomato mixture. Add the lid then cook on low for 8–10 hours. Spoon on to plates and serve on a bed of mashed potatoes or polenta.

Tip
• **To cook quick-cook polenta, simply stir it into boiling water, cook for 1–2 minutes until thick then add butter, a little grated Parmesan cheese and plenty of salt and pepper.**

Hungarian goulash

Goulash is often considered a mild stew although a true Hungarian goulash can be quite fiery since the paprika available in Eastern Europe comes in four strengths. Combine paprika with chilli powder to taste for a hotter dish. Serve with warmed sauerkraut or plain boiled potatoes.

Serves 4

Preparation time: 25 minutes
Cooking time: 8–10 hours
Cooking temperature: low
Slow cooker size: standard

1 tablespoon sunflower oil
700 g (1 lb 6 oz) pork, diced
1 large onion, chopped
150 g (5 oz) button mushrooms, halved
2 teaspoons paprika, plus extra to garnish
1/4 teaspoon ground cinnamon
1/4 teaspoon ground allspice
1 teaspoon caraway seeds
2 tablespoons plain flour
400 g (13 oz) can chopped tomatoes
450 ml (3/4 pint) hot chicken stock
salt and pepper
soured cream, to serve

1 Preheat the slow cooker if necessary – see manufacturer's instructions. Heat the oil in a frying pan then add the pork, a few pieces at a time, until it has all been added to the pan. Stir in the onion and cook for 5 minutes until lightly browned.

2 Add the mushrooms and cook for 2 minutes. Stir in the spices and the flour and cook for 1 minute. Mix in the canned tomatoes then bring the mixture to the boil.

3 Transfer the mixture to the slow cooker pot. Stir in the stock and season with salt and pepper, cover with the lid and cook on low for 8–10 hours.

4 Spoon the goulash on to plates, top with spoonfuls of soured cream and sprinkle with a little extra paprika.

Tip
• **To make in a larger slow cooker, increase the ingredient quantities by half as much again and cook for the same length of time.**

85

Pork, orange & star anise

This is a great everyday casserole, which avoids being ordinary by adding a hint of oriental spice and mellow-tasting plum sauce. It's delicious served with mashed potatoes mixed with green vegetables.

Serves 4

Preparation time: 20 minutes
Cooking time: 8–10 hours
Cooking temperature: low
Slow cooker size: standard

1 tablespoon sunflower oil
4 pork shoulder steaks or boneless spare rib chops, about 700 g (1 lb 7 oz), each cut into 3
1 onion, chopped
2 tablespoons plain flour
450 ml (¾ pint) chicken stock
grated rind and juice of 1 orange
3 tablespoons plum sauce
2 tablespoons soy sauce
3–4 whole star anise
1 fresh or dried red chilli, halved (optional)
salt and pepper
grated orange rind, to garnish

To serve
mashed potatoes mixed with steamed green vegetables, such as peas and cabbage

1 Preheat the slow cooker if necessary – see manufacturer's instructions. Heat the oil in a large frying pan, add the pieces of pork and fry over a high heat until browned on both sides. Lift the pork out of the pan with a slotted spoon and transfer to a plate.

2 Add the onion to the pan and fry, stirring, for 5 minutes or until lightly browned. Stir in the flour, then mix in the stock, orange rind and juice, plum sauce, soy sauce, star anise and chilli, if using. Season with salt and pepper and bring to the boil, stirring.

3 Transfer the pork to the slow cooker pot and pour the sauce over it. Cover and cook on low for 8–10 hours. Serve with mashed potatoes mixed with steamed green vegetables and garnish with grated orange rind.

Tips
- **Warn diners not to eat the star anise.**
- **If you don't have any star anise, use a cinnamon stick, broken in half.**
- **If you like garlic, add 2 cloves, finely chopped, just after frying the onions.**

Glazed gammon
with split pea purée

Serves 4

Preparation time: 30 minutes, plus soaking
Cooking time: 6–7 hours
Cooking temperature: high
Slow cooker size: standard

1.25 kg (2½ lb) boneless smoked gammon joint
200 g (7 oz) dried yellow split peas
1 large onion, roughly chopped
2 carrots, sliced
5 cloves
2 bay leaves
1.2 litres (2 pints) water

To glaze

2 teaspoons Dijon mustard
2 tablespoons maple syrup

1 Put the gammon joint in a bowl, cover with cold water and transfer to the refrigerator. Put the split peas in a second bowl, cover with cold water and leave at room temperature. Soak both overnight.

2 Preheat the slow cooker if necessary – see manufacturer's instructions. Drain the peas and put them in a saucepan with the onion, carrots, cloves, bay leaves and the measured water. Bring to the boil and boil rapidly for 10 minutes, skimming off any scum.

3 Drain the gammon joint and put it in the slow cooker pot. Pour the water and pea mixture over the top, cover and cook on high for 6–7 hours or until the peas are soft and the gammon is tender.

4 Lift the gammon out of the pot, put it in a grill pan and cut away the rind. Spread the mustard over the fat, then drizzle with the maple syrup. Cook under the grill until the fat is golden.

5 Meanwhile, drain off most of the stock from the peas but reserve the liquid. Mash the peas and spoon them on to plates. Slice the gammon and arrange on top, and serve with a little of the reserved ham stock if liked.

Tip
• **You can use honey to glaze the gammon if you do not have any maple syrup.**

Bigos

Popular in eastern Europe, this pork casserole is flavoured with sauerkraut, paprika and caraway seeds and served with chunky pieces of pork, smoked pork sausage and pickled cucumbers.

Serves 4

Preparation time: 30 minutes
Cooking time: 8–10 hours
Cooking temperature: low
Slow cooker size: standard

625 g (1¼ lb) lean pork belly
1 tablespoon sunflower oil
1 large onion, roughly chopped
1 teaspoon paprika
1 teaspoon caraway seeds
400 g (13 oz) can chopped tomatoes
450 ml (¾ pint) chicken stock
2 dessert apples, cored and diced (skins left on)
225 g (7½ oz) smoked pork sausage, thickly sliced
150 g (5 oz) pickled dill cucumbers, drained and
  thickly sliced
375 g (12 oz) sauerkraut, drained
salt and pepper
bread, to serve

1 Preheat the slow cooker if necessary – see manufacturer's instructions. Remove the rind from the pork belly and dice the meat. Heat the oil in a large frying pan, add the onion and pork and fry until lightly browned.

2 Stir in the paprika and caraway seeds, then mix in the tomatoes and stock. Season to taste with salt and pepper and bring to the boil, stirring.

3 Put the apples, smoked pork sausage and dill cucumbers into the slow cooker pot. Pour over the pork and onion mixture, then spoon the sauerkraut on top. Cover and cook on low for 8–10 hours.

4 Stir and spoon into shallow bowls. Serve with bread and spoons to scoop up the sauce.

Tip
• **The pork sausage, which is shaped like a horseshoe, is sometimes known as smoked pork boiling ring. If you cannot get this use a spiced sausage such as *kabanos*.**

Pot-roasted chicken

A whole chicken can be very successfully cooked in a slow cooker. By starting the bird breast side down, the breast stays more moist and, unlike oven roasting, it won't come to any harm if for some reason the dinner gets delayed.

Serves 4–5

Preparation time: 25 minutes
Cooking time: 5–6 hours
Cooking temperature: high
Slow cooker size: large or extra large

1.5 kg (3 lb) whole chicken
2 tablespoons olive oil
1 large onion, cut into 6 wedges
500 ml (17 fl oz) dry cider
3 teaspoons Dijon mustard
2 teaspoons caster sugar
900 ml (1½ pints) hot chicken stock
3 carrots, cut into chunky pieces
3 celery sticks, thickly sliced
1 lemon, cut into 6 wedges
20 g (¾ oz) fresh tarragon
3 tablespoons crème fraîche
salt and pepper
lemon wedges, to garnish (optional)

1 Preheat the slow cooker if necessary – see manufacturer's instructions. Wash the chicken inside and out with cold water then pat dry with kitchen paper. Heat the oil in a large frying pan, add the chicken, breast side down, and fry for 10 minutes, turning the chicken several times until it is browned all over.

2 Carefully put the chicken, breast side down, in the slow cooker pot. Fry the onion wedges in the remaining oil in the pan until lightly browned. Add the cider, mustard, sugar and season with salt and pepper and bring to the boil. Pour over the chicken, add the hot stock then add the vegetables, lemon wedges and 3 sprigs of the tarragon. Make sure the chicken and vegetables are well below the level of the stock so they cook evenly and thoroughly.

3 Cover with the cooker lid and cook the chicken on high for 5–6 hours until it is thoroughly cooked and the meat juices run clear when the thickest parts of the leg and breast are pierced with a sharp knife. Turn the chicken after 4 hours, if liked.

4 Lift the chicken out of the stock, drain well and transfer to a large serving plate. Remove the vegetables using a slotted spoon and arrange them around the chicken. Measure 600 ml (1 pint) of the hot cooking stock from the slow cooker pot into a jug. Reserve a few sprigs of tarragon to garnish, chop the remainder and whisk into the stock with the crème fraîche to make a gravy. Adjust the seasoning to taste. Carve the chicken in the usual way and serve with the gravy and vegetables. Garnish with fresh lemon wedges, if liked, and the reserved tarragon sprigs.

with lemon

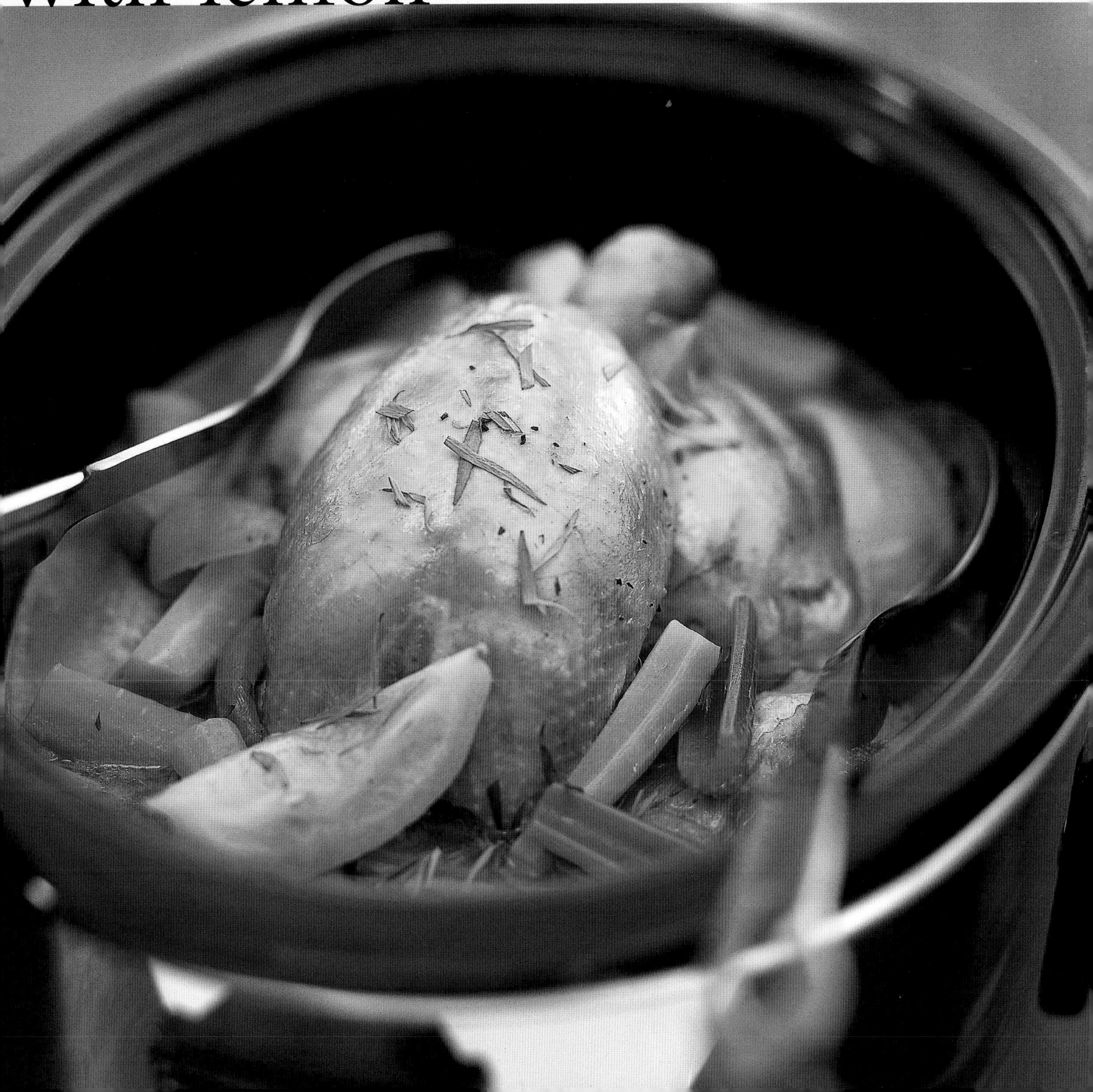

Spanish chicken pot

Spicy chorizo adds an authentic Mediterranean flavour to an everyday chicken casserole. Buy the sausage whole from the delicatessen counter and dice it yourself as it has much more flavour than packets of wafer-thin ready-sliced chorizo.

Serves 6–8

Preparation time: 30 minutes
Cooking time: 8–10 hours
Cooking temperature: low
Slow cooker size: large or extra large

2 tablespoons olive oil
6 chicken thighs, skinned if liked
6 chicken drumsticks, skinned if liked
1 large slice of onion
2–3 garlic cloves, chopped
3 tablespoons plain flour
2 x 400 g (13 oz) cans chopped tomatoes
150 g (5 oz) piece of chorizo sausage, diced
750 g (1½ lb) baby new potatoes, scrubbed and
    halved or quartered depending on size
450 ml (¾ pint) hot chicken stock
65 g (2½ oz) pitted black olives
a few fresh rosemary sprigs or a pinch of dried
salt and pepper
basil or extra rosemary sprigs, to garnish
crusty bread, to serve

1 Preheat the slow cooker if necessary – see manufacturer's instructions. Heat the oil in a large frying pan and fry the chicken in batches until browned on all sides. Drain and transfer to a large plate.

2 Add the onion to the pan and fry for 5 minutes until pale golden. Stir in the garlic then the flour. Add the canned tomatoes and chorizo and season with salt and pepper. Bring to the boil.

3 Transfer the chicken and potatoes to the slow cooker pot, pour in the tomato mixture then add the hot stock, olives and rosemary. Cover with the lid and cook on low for 8–10 hours.

4 Spoon into shallow dishes, sprinkle with fresh rosemary or basil and serve with plenty of warm crusty bread to dunk into the delicious sauce.

Tips

- **To make in a smaller slow cooker, halve the ingredient quantities and cook for the same length of time.**

- **If you have any wine already opened, you may like to substitute this for a little of the chicken stock.**

Persian chicken

Serves 4

Preparation time: 30 minutes
Cooking time: 8¼–9¼ hours
Cooking temperature: low
Slow cooker size: standard

4 chicken drumsticks, skinned
4 chicken thighs, skinned
2 tablespoons plain flour
1 teaspoon turmeric
1 teaspoon paprika
2 tablespoons olive oil
1 large onion, chopped
2 garlic cloves, chopped (optional)
4 cloves
2.5 cm (1 inch) fresh root ginger, finely chopped
450 ml (¾ pint) chicken stock
125 g (4 oz) young spinach, well washed, larger
    leaves torn into pieces
salt and pepper
couscous, to serve

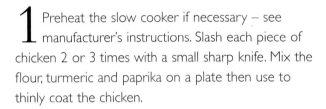

1 Preheat the slow cooker if necessary – see manufacturer's instructions. Slash each piece of chicken 2 or 3 times with a small sharp knife. Mix the flour, turmeric and paprika on a plate then use to thinly coat the chicken.

2 Heat the oil in a frying pan, add the chicken and cook until browned on both sides. Transfer to a plate. Add the onion and garlic, if using, to the pan and fry, stirring, for 5 minutes until lightly browned.

3 Stir in any remaining spiced flour. Add the cloves, ginger, stock and salt and pepper to taste and bring to the boil, stirring.

4 Pack the chicken joints into the slow cooker pot then pour in the onion mixture. Cover with the lid and cook on low for 8–9 hours until the chicken is tender. Add the spinach and cook for 15 minutes more, then serve the chicken on a bed of couscous.

& chicken pilaf

Whole chicken breasts are flavoured with a rich sun-dried tomato sauce and braised on a base of wild and basmati rice. Serve with rocket leaves tossed in an olive oil and lemon dressing for an easy supper.

Serves 4

Preparation time: 25 minutes
Cooking time: 3–4 hours
Cooking temperature: high
Slow cooker size: standard

1 tablespoon olive oil
4 boneless, skinless chicken breasts
1 large onion, roughly chopped
2 garlic cloves, chopped (optional)
400 g (13 oz) can chopped tomatoes
50 g (2 oz) sun-dried tomatoes in oil, drained
   and sliced
2 teaspoons pesto
600 ml (1 pint) hot chicken stock
150 g (5 oz) basmati rice
50 g (2 oz) wild rice
salt and pepper
rocket salad, to serve

1 Preheat the slow cooker if necessary – see manufacturer's instructions. Heat the oil in a frying pan then fry the chicken breasts on one side only until browned. Remove from the pan with a slotted spoon and reserve on a plate.

2 Fry the onion and garlic, if using, in the pan for 5 minutes, stirring until lightly browned. Add the canned tomatoes, sun-dried tomatoes and pesto, season with salt and pepper and bring to the boil. Pour into the slow cooker pot then stir in the stock.

3 Rinse the basmati rice well in a sieve under cold running water, then stir into the slow cooker pot with the wild rice. Arrange the chicken breasts on top of the rice, browned side uppermost, pressing them just below the level of the liquid so that they don't dry out during cooking. Cover with the lid and cook on high for 3–4 hours until the chicken is thoroughly cooked and the rice is tender.

4 Spoon on to serving plates and serve with a rocket salad.

Tip
- **The dish will not come to any harm if left to cook for longer than the time specified, although you will need to top up the pot with a little extra hot chicken stock.**

Lemon chicken

Whole chicken breasts are gently simmered with garlic and lemon wedges and finished with pak choi, sugar snap peas and minted crème fraîche. They're delicious served with a couscous salad.

Serves 4

Preparation time: 20 minutes
Cooking time: 3¼–4¼ hours
Cooking temperature: high
Slow cooker size: standard

1 tablespoon olive oil
4 boneless, skinless chicken breasts, about
  550 g (1 lb 2 oz)
1 onion, chopped
2 garlic cloves, finely chopped
2 tablespoons plain flour
450 ml (¾ pint) chicken stock
½ lemon (cut in half lengthways), cut into 4 wedges
2 pak choi, thickly sliced
125 g (4 oz) sugar snap peas, halved lengthways
4 tablespoons crème fraîche
2 tablespoons chopped mint and parsley mixed
salt and pepper
couscous salad, to serve

1 Preheat the slow cooker if necessary – see manufacturer's instructions. Heat the oil in a large frying pan, add the chicken breasts and fry over a high heat until browned on both sides. Remove from the pan and transfer to a plate. Add the onion to the pan and fry, stirring, for 5 minutes or until lightly browned.

2 Stir in the garlic and flour, then mix in the stock and lemon wedges. Season with salt and pepper and bring to the boil.

3 Put the chicken breasts in the slow cooker pot, pour the hot stock mixture over them and press the chicken below the surface of the liquid. Cover and cook on high for 3–4 hours.

4 Add the pak choi and sugar snap peas and cook on high for 15 minutes or until just tender. Lift out the chicken, slice the pieces and arrange them on plates. Stir the crème fraîche and herbs into the sauce, then spoon it and the vegetables over the chicken. Serve with couscous mixed with finely chopped tomato, red onion and red pepper.

Kashmiri butter chicken

This mild, delicately fragrant curry has a rich creamy sauce that is sure to please all your guests, no matter what their preferences. Serve it with plain boiled rice or warm naan bread.

Serves 4

Preparation time: 30 minutes
Cooking time: 5–7 hours
Cooking temperature: low
Slow cooker size: standard

2 onions, quartered
3 garlic cloves
4 cm (1½ inch) fresh root ginger, peeled
1 large red chilli, halved, seeds discarded
8 boneless, skinless chicken thighs
1 tablespoon sunflower oil
25 g (1 oz) butter
1 teaspoon cumin seeds, crushed
1 teaspoon fennel seeds, crushed
4 cardamom pods, crushed
1 teaspoon paprika
1 teaspoon ground turmeric
¼ teaspoon ground cinnamon
300 ml (½ pint) chicken stock
1 tablespoon light muscovado sugar
2 tablespoons tomato purée
5 tablespoons double cream
salt

To garnish
2 tablespoons flaked almonds, toasted
sprigs of coriander

1 Preheat the slow cooker if necessary – see manufacturer's instructions. Blend the onions, garlic, ginger and chilli in a food processor or liquidizer or chop finely.

2 Cut each chicken thigh into 4 pieces. Heat the oil in a large frying pan and add the chicken, a few pieces at a time, until all the meat has been added. Cook over a high heat until evenly browned. Lift the chicken pieces out of the pan with a slotted spoon and transfer to a plate.

3 Add the butter to the frying pan and when it has melted add the onion paste. Cook over a more moderate heat until it is just beginning to colour. Stir in the crushed seeds, cardamom seeds and pods and ground spices. Cook for 1 minute, then mix in the stock, sugar, tomato purée and salt. Bring to the boil, stirring.

4 Transfer the chicken to the slow cooker pot, pour the onion mixture and sauce over the top and press the pieces of chicken below the surface of the liquid. Cover and cook on low for 5–7 hours.

5 Stir in the cream and serve garnished with toasted flaked almonds and sprigs of coriander.

Frikadeller

These Danish meatballs, which are cooked in a deep yellow mustard sauce, can be made with minced pork instead of turkey if you prefer. Serve them in shallow bowls with creamy mashed potatoes or celeriac, a side dish of diced dill cucumbers and a spoon to scoop up the delicious sauce.

Serves 4

Preparation time: 30 minutes
Cooking time: 6–8 hours
Cooking temperature: low
Slow cooker size: standard

Meatballs

1 onion, finely chopped
500 g (1 lb) minced turkey
50 g (2 oz) fresh white breadcrumbs
1 egg yolk
1 tablespoon sunflower oil
salt and pepper

Sauce

50 g (2 oz) butter
1 onion, finely chopped
40 g (1½ oz) plain flour
600 ml (1 pint) chicken stock
3 teaspoons mild Swedish or Dijon mustard
½ teaspoon ground turmeric

To serve

Mashed potatoes
sprigs of flat leaf parsley

1 Preheat the slow cooker if necessary – see manufacturer's instructions. Make the meatballs. Mix together the onion, turkey, breadcrumbs, egg yolk and plenty of salt and pepper in a mixing bowl. Wet your hands and shape the mixture into 20 small meatballs.

2 Heat the oil in a large frying pan, add the meatballs and cook over a high heat, turning until evenly browned. Lift them out with a slotted spoon and transfer to a plate.

3 Make the sauce. Melt the butter in a clean frying pan, add the onion and fry gently for 5 minutes or until softened. Stir in the flour, then gradually mix in the stock and bring to the boil, stirring until smooth. Stir in the mustard and turmeric and season with salt and pepper.

4 Transfer the meatballs to the slow cooker pot, pour the sauce over them, then cover and cook on low for 6–8 hours. Serve with mashed potatoes and garnish with flat leaf parsley.

Turkey carbonnade
with polenta squares

Serves 4

Preparation time: 30 minutes
Cooking time: 8–10 hours
Cooking temperature: low
Slow cooker size: standard

1 tablespoon olive oil
500 g (1 lb) minced turkey
1 large onion, roughly chopped
2 garlic cloves, finely chopped
1 large carrot, diced
2 tablespoons plain flour
400 g (13 oz) can chopped tomatoes
300 ml (½ pint) chicken stock
50 g (2 oz) sun-dried tomatoes, drained and
   thickly sliced
2–3 sprigs of rosemary
salt and pepper
rocket salad, to serve

Polenta

850 ml (30 fl oz) boiling water
150 g (5 oz) quick-cook polenta
50 g (2 oz) butter
3 tablespoons grated Parmesan cheese, plus
   extra to garnish
2 tablespoons olive oil

1 Preheat the slow cooker if necessary – see manufacturer's instructions. Heat the oil in a large frying pan, add the meat and onion and fry over a high heat, stirring, for 5 minutes or until browned. Stir in the garlic and carrot and cook for 2 minutes.

2 Mix in the flour, then add the canned tomatoes, stock, sun-dried tomatoes and rosemary. Season with salt and pepper and bring to the boil, stirring to break up any large clumps of mince. Spoon the mixture into the slow cooker pot, press the mince below the surface of the liquid, cover and cook on low for 8–10 hours.

3 Prepare the polenta. Bring the measured water to the boil in a saucepan, add the polenta, bring back to the boil and cook, stirring, for 1–2 minutes or until thick. Remove from the heat, add the butter, Parmesan and plenty of salt and pepper and stir until the butter has melted. Pour into an oiled 20 cm (8 inch) shallow cake tin or small roasting tin, spread into an even layer and leave to cool and set.

4 Cut the polenta into 12 pieces, heat the oil in a large frying pan and fry the polenta until it is hot and golden. Arrange pieces on a serving plate, overlapping around the edge of the mince, sprinkle with a little extra Parmesan and serve with a rocket salad.

Summer garden pie

This comforting midweek supper dish is made with diced chicken thighs, which are simmered with diced bacon and wholegrain mustard and then finished with a colourful mix of fresh seasonal vegetables topped with tasty mustard mashed potatoes.

Serves 6

Preparation time: 30 minutes
Cooking time: 6 hours 20 minutes–8 hours 20 minutes
Cooking temperature: low and high
Slow cooker size: standard

8 chicken thighs, about 1 kg (2 lb) in total
1 tablespoon sunflower oil
1 onion, chopped
2 rashers of smoked back bacon, diced
2 tablespoons plain flour
450 ml (¾ pint) chicken stock
2 teaspoons wholegrain mustard
2 carrots, diced
2 courgettes, diced
150 g (5 oz) runner beans, cut into thin strips
100 g (3½ oz) fresh or frozen peas
salt and pepper

Mustard mash

1 kg (2 lb) potatoes
40 g (1½ oz) butter
2–4 tablespoons milk
2 teaspoons wholegrain mustard
40 g (1½ oz) strong Cheddar cheese, grated

1 Preheat the slow cooker if necessary – see manufacturer's instructions. Cut the skin away from the chicken thighs, remove the bones and cut the meat into chunks.

2 Heat the oil in a large frying pan, add the chicken, a few pieces at a time, until all the meat is in the pan, then add the onion and bacon. Fry, stirring, for 5 minutes or until lightly browned.

3 Mix in the flour, then add the stock, mustard and carrots. Season to taste with salt and pepper, bring to the boil and transfer to the slow cooker pot. Cover and cook on low for 6–8 hours.

4 Add the green vegetables to the slow cooker, replace the lid and cook on high for 20 minutes or until tender.

5 Meanwhile, cook the potatoes in a saucepan of boiling water until tender. Drain and mash with the butter and milk. Stir in the mustard and salt and pepper to taste. Spoon the potato over the top of the slow cooker pot and sprinkle with the cheese. Grill, if liked, to brown the top of the pie.

Caribbean chicken

with rice & peas

There are as many versions of rice and peas as there are types of peas and beans. Here red kidney beans, white long-grain rice and frozen green peas are added to chicken thighs spread with spicy jerk marinade and simmered in coconut milk.

Serves 4
Preparation time: 20 minutes
Cooking time: 7–9 hours
Cooking temperature: low and high
Slow cooker size: standard

8 chicken thighs, about 1 kg (2 lb)
3 tablespoons jerk marinade (see tip below)
2 tablespoons sunflower oil
2 large onions, chopped
2 garlic cloves, finely chopped
400 ml (14 fl oz) can coconut milk
300 ml (½ pint) chicken stock
410 g (13½ oz) can red kidney beans, drained
200 g (7 oz) easy-cook, white long-grain rice
125 g (4 oz) frozen peas
salt and pepper

To garnish
lime wedges
coriander sprigs

1 Preheat the slow cooker if necessary – see manufacturer's instructions. Remove the skin from the chicken thighs, slash each thigh two or three times and rub with the jerk marinade.

2 Heat 1 tablespoon oil in a large frying pan, add the chicken and fry over a high heat until browned on both sides. Lift out and transfer to a plate. Add the remaining oil, the onions and garlic, reduce the heat and fry for 5 minutes or until softened and lightly browned. Pour in the coconut milk and stock, season with salt and pepper and bring the mixture to the boil.

3 Transfer half the mixture to the slow cooker pot, add half the chicken pieces, all the beans and then the remaining chicken, onions and coconut mixture. Cover and cook on low for 6–8 hours or until the chicken is tender.

4 Stir in the rice, replace the lid and cook on high for 45 minutes. Add the frozen peas (no need to defrost) and cook for 15 minutes more. Spoon on to plates and garnish with lime wedges and coriander sprigs.

Tip
• Jerk marinade is a spicy dark brown paste, and you will find jars of it in most large supermarkets.

Peppered venison

Serves 4–5

Preparation time: 35 minutes
Cooking time: 8¾–11 hours
Cooking temperature: low and high
Slow cooker size: standard

25 g (1 oz) butter
1 tablespoon olive oil
750 g (1½ lb) venison shoulder, diced
1 large red onion, sliced
125 g (4 oz) cup mushrooms, sliced
2 garlic cloves, finely chopped (optional)
2 tablespoons plain flour
200 ml (7 fl oz) red wine
250 ml (8 fl oz) lamb or chicken stock
2 teaspoons tomato purée
2 tablespoons redcurrant jelly
1 teaspoon peppercorns, roughly crushed
salt and pepper
green beans, to serve

Scones

250 g (8 oz) self-raising flour
40 g (1½ oz) butter, diced
125 g (4 oz) Gorgonzola cheese, rind removed
  and diced
3 tablespoons chopped parsley or chives
1 egg, beaten
4–5 tablespoons milk

1 Preheat the slow cooker if necessary – see manufacturer's instructions. Heat the butter and oil in a large frying pan, add the diced venison, a few pieces at time, until all the meat has been added, then fry until evenly browned. Transfer to a plate.

2 Add the onion and fry for 5 minutes. Stir in the mushrooms, garlic, if using, and flour and cook for 1 minute. Stir in the wine, stock, tomato purée, redcurrant jelly, peppercorns and salt and bring to the boil.

3 Spoon the venison into the pot, add the hot wine mixture and press the venison below the surface. Cover and cook on low for 8–10 hours.

4 Make the scones. Place the flour in a bowl, add the butter and rub in with the fingertips until the mixture resembles fine breadcrumbs. Stir in a little salt and pepper, the cheese and herbs. Reserve 1 tablespoon of egg for glazing and add the rest. Gradually mix in enough milk to make a soft dough.

5 Lightly knead, then pat the dough into a thick oval or round that is a little smaller than the top of your slow cooker. Cut it into 8 wedges and arrange, spaced slightly apart, on top of the venison. Cover and cook on high for 45 minutes–1 hour.

6 Brush the scones with the reserved egg and brown under the grill. Serve with green beans.

with Gorgonzola scones

Turkey chilli
with chocolate

Mexican cooks have long used dark chocolate in savoury dishes – it combines unusually well with chicken or turkey, and with chilli. Serve with tortillas or rice and a side salad.

Serves 4

Preparation time: 25 minutes
Cooking time: 8–10 hours
Cooking temperature: low
Slow cooker size: standard

1 tablespoon sunflower oil
500 g (1 lb) minced turkey
1 large onion, chopped
2 garlic cloves, chopped
½–1 teaspoon chilli powder
1 teaspoon cumin seeds, roughly crushed
½ teaspoon ground cinnamon
¼ teaspoon ground cloves
1 tablespoon plain flour
410 g (13½ oz) can red kidney beans,
   drained and rinsed
400 g (13 oz) can chopped tomatoes
450 ml (¾ pint) chicken stock
1 tablespoon tomato purée
25 g (1 oz) dark chocolate, chopped
salt and pepper

To serve

4 soft tortillas
guacamole (see Tip)
4 tablespoons soured cream

1 Preheat the slow cooker if necessary – see manufacturer's instructions. Heat the oil in a frying pan, add the turkey mince and onion and fry, stirring, for 5 minutes until browned. Stir in the garlic, spices and flour then add the kidney beans, canned tomatoes, stock, tomato purée, chocolate and season with salt and pepper.

2 Bring to the boil, breaking up any large pieces of mince, then transfer the mixture to the slow cooker pot. Cover with the lid and cook on low for 8–10 hours. Stir well and serve in warmed soft tortillas topped with guacamole and spoonfuls of soured cream.

Tips

- **If you have an extra large slow cooker, simply double the ingredient quantities and cook for the same length of time.**

- **To make guacamole, halve an avocado and remove the stone, scoop out the flesh with a spoon then mash with fresh lime or lemon juice and season with salt and pepper.**

Venison sausage & lentil stew

Serves 4

Preparation time: 20 minutes
Cooking time: 6–7 hours
Cooking temperature: low
Slow cooker size: standard

1 tablespoon olive oil
8 venison sausages
1 large onion, chopped
2 garlic cloves, chopped (optional)
2 tablespoons plain flour
900 ml (1½ pints) chicken stock
3 tablespoons brown sugar
2 tablespoons tomato purée
2 tablespoons balsamic vinegar
200 g (7 oz) puy lentils
250 g (8 oz) cranberries, defrosted if frozen
2 bay leaves
salt and pepper
crusty bread, to serve

1 Preheat the slow cooker if necessary – see manufacturer's instructions. Heat the oil in a frying pan, add the sausages and fry over a high heat until browned, but not cooked through. Transfer to a plate.

2 Add the onion to the pan and fry, stirring, until lightly browned. Add the garlic, if using, then the flour. Stir in the stock, sugar, tomato purée and vinegar, season with salt and pepper and bring to the boil.

3 Put the lentils, cranberries and bay leaves in the slow cooker pot, pour in the hot stock mixture then add the sausages. Cover with the lid and cook on low for 6–7 hours. Stir well then spoon into shallow dishes, discarding the bay leaves, and serve with warm crusty bread.

This makes a smart dinner party dish. Creamy gratin Dauphinois and green beans are good accompaniments.

Serves 4

Preparation time: 35 minutes
Cooking time: 2–2½ hours
Cooking temperature: low
Slow cooker size: standard

4 pheasant breasts, about 600 g (1 lb 3 oz)
small bunch of sage
100 g (3½ oz) packet sliced smoked pancetta
25 g (1 oz) butter
200 g (7 oz) shallots, halved if large
2 tablespoons plain flour
150 ml (¼ pint) dry cider
150 ml (¼ pint) chicken stock
1 teaspoon Dijon mustard
1 dessert apple, cored and sliced
240 g (7¾ oz) can whole peeled chestnuts, drained
salt and pepper
carrots, to serve
chopped parsley, to garnish

1 Preheat the slow cooker if necessary – see manufacturer's instructions. Rinse the pheasant breasts with cold water, pat dry with kitchen paper then season well with salt and pepper. Top each breast with a few sage leaves then wrap in sliced pancetta until completely covered. Tie at intervals with fine string to keep the pancetta in place.

2 Heat the butter in a frying pan, add the shallots and fry for 4–5 minutes until browned. Stir in the flour then add the cider, stock and mustard. Add the apple and chestnuts and a little extra salt and pepper then bring to the boil, stirring.

3 Arrange the pheasant breasts in the slow cooker pot. Pour the hot onion mixture over the top. Cover with the lid and cook on low for 2½–3 hours until the pheasant is tender. Spoon on to plates, remove the string from the pheasant and serve with carrots, garnished with chopped parsley.

Tip
- **Chicken breasts may be wrapped and cooked in the same way. Unlike pheasant breasts, they do not dry out as readily, so they can be left in the slow cooker for 5–6 hours without spoiling if you are delayed.**

Cheat's game pie

Serves 6

Preparation time: 45 minutes
Cooking time: 8½–9½ hours
Cooking temperature: low
Slow cooker size: standard

15 g (½ oz) butter
1 tablespoon olive oil
1 cock pheasant, jointed
1 chicken leg, separated into drumstick
   and thigh joints
340 g (11½ oz) diced venison
1 large onion, chopped
100 g (3½ oz) smoked streaky bacon,
   rinded and diced
3 tablespoons brandy
200 ml (7 fl oz) red wine
300 ml (½ pint) chicken stock
2 teaspoons juniper berries
3 bay leaves
1 tablespoon tomato purée
4 teaspoons cornflour
salt and pepper

Pastry circles
500 g (1 lb) puff pastry, defrosted if frozen
beaten egg, to glaze
coarse sea salt, for sprinkling

1 Preheat the slow cooker if necessary – see manufacturer's instructions. Heat the butter and oil in a frying pan, add the pheasant and chicken joints and fry until browned all over. Transfer to a plate.

2 Add the venison, onion and bacon to the pan and fry for 5 minutes, stirring until browned. Add the brandy, bring to the boil then flame with a match taking care to stand well back. When the flames have subsided, stir in the red wine, stock, juniper berries, bay leaves, tomato purée and season with salt and pepper. Bring to the boil, stirring.

3 Arrange the pheasant and chicken in the slow cooker pot. Pour in the venison and onion mixture. Cover with the lid and cook on low for 8–9 hours until tender.

4 Remove the pheasant and chicken from the slow cooker pot, but keep the slow cooker switched on. Take the meat off the bones and return to the pot. Mix the cornflour to a smooth paste with a little cold water then stir into the casserole. Replace the lid and cook for another 30 minutes.

5 Meanwhile, roll out the pastry thinly on a lightly floured surface and cut out 6 × 12 cm (5 inch) circles. Place on a greased baking tray. Cut decorative leaf shapes from any trimmings and arrange on top of the pastry circles. Brush the pastry with egg, sprinkle with salt and bake in a preheated oven, 200°C (400°F), Gas Mark 6, for 8–10 minutes until well risen and golden.

6 Spoon the game casserole on to serving plates, discarding the bay leaves, and top with the pastry circles to serve.

Cassoulet

This French so-called 'peasant food' is made in the classic way with beans, diced pork, spicy sausage, tomatoes and rough red wine. Duck has been used instead of the traditional, more expensive goose.

Serves 4

Preparation time: 30 minutes
Cooking time: 8–9 hours
Cooking temperature: low
Slow cooker size: standard

4 small duck legs
250 g (8 oz) lean pork belly rashers, rind removed, diced
1 large onion, chopped
2–3 garlic cloves, chopped
2 tablespoons plain flour
400 g (13 oz) can chopped tomatoes
200 ml (7 fl oz) red wine
100 ml (3½ fl oz) chicken stock
1 tablespoon brown sugar
2 teaspoons Dijon mustard
2 x 410 g (13½ oz) cans mixed beans, drained and rinsed
125 g (4 oz) piece of chorizo sausage, diced
1 fresh or dried bouquet garni
40 g (1½ oz) fresh breadcrumbs
salt and pepper
green salad, to serve

1 Preheat the slow cooker if necessary – see manufacturer's instructions. Dry-fry the duck legs in a frying pan until browned all over. Transfer to a plate. Pour off all but 1 tablespoon duck fat from the pan.

2 Add the diced pork and onion to the pan and fry for 5 minutes, stirring until lightly browned. Stir in the garlic and flour. Add the canned tomatoes, wine, stock, sugar and mustard. Season with salt and pepper and bring to the boil, stirring.

3 Pour half the drained beans into the slow cooker pot. Arrange the duck pieces, chorizo and bouquet garni on top. Add the remaining beans then pour in the pork and tomato mixture. Sprinkle with the breadcrumbs then cover with the lid and cook on low for 8–9 hours. Spoon on to plates and serve with a green salad.

Tip

• **If your slow cooker has a maximum working capacity of less than 2.5 litres (4 pints) then use 2 halved duck breasts and an extra 250 g (8 oz) diced pork belly, otherwise the mixture will not fit in the pot.**

Pot-roast guinea

Serves 4

Preparation time: 30 minutes
Cooking time: 5¼–6¼ hours
Cooking temperature: high
Slow cooker size: standard

1 tablespoon olive oil
25 g (1 oz) butter
1 guinea fowl, about 1 kg (2 lb)
1 large onion, cut into thin wedges
2 leeks, thickly sliced (keep white and green
   slices separate)
2 garlic cloves, finely chopped
200 ml (7 fl oz) dry white wine
2 teaspoons Dijon mustard
500 g (1 lb) baby new potatoes, thickly sliced
200 g (7 oz) carrots, sliced
900 ml (1½ pints) hot chicken stock
150 g (5 oz) hulled broad beans, thawed if frozen
salt and pepper

Salsa verde
25 g (1 oz) flat leaf parsley, chopped
2 garlic cloves, finely chopped
3 tablespoons olive oil
2 teaspoons white wine vinegar

1 Preheat the slow cooker if necessary – see manufacturer's instructions. Heat the oil and butter in a frying pan, add the guinea fowl breast side downwards and fry until golden. Turn and brown the underside. Lift out and put on to a plate.

2 Add the onion and white sliced leeks and fry for 5 minutes. Add the garlic and cook for 2 minutes, then stir in the wine and mustard, season with salt and pepper, and bring to the boil.

3 Put the guinea fowl into the slow cooker pot, breast side uppermost. Tuck the potatoes and carrots down the sides of the bird. Pour over the hot onion, leek and wine mixture, then add the hot stock. Make sure that the potatoes and carrots are below the stock level. Cover and cook on high for 5–6 hours or until the guinea fowl and vegetables are tender. Check the guinea fowl by inserting a knife through the thickest part of the leg into the breast meat. The juices will run clear when the bird is ready.

4 Lift the guinea fowl out of the pot, put it on a plate and wrap in foil to keep hot. Add the green sliced leeks and broad beans to the pot and cook on high for 15 minutes. Meanwhile, mix together the salsa verde ingredients in a small bowl.

5 Spoon the vegetables and some of the stock into serving bowls. Carve the guinea fowl and add it to the bowls with spoonfuls of salsa verde.

fowl with salsa verde

Vegetable dishes

& brown bean salad

Amazingly tasty and yet made with just a few ingredients, this salad is served here as a vegetarian main course but it could also be served in smaller portions as a delicious first course.

Serves 4–5

Preparation time: 25 minutes
Cooking time: 3½–4½ hours
Cooking temperature: low
Slow cooker size: standard

1 tablespoon olive oil
1 large onion, chopped
500 g (1 lb) raw beetroot, peeled and finely diced
2 x 410 g (13½ oz) cans borlotti beans, drained and rinsed
450 ml (¾ pint) vegetable stock
salt and pepper

To serve

¼ cucumber, finely diced
200 g (7 oz) natural yogurt
1 cos or iceberg lettuce
4 red- or white-stemmed spring onions, thinly sliced
4 tablespoons chopped coriander or mint leaves
salt and pepper

1 Preheat the slow cooker if necessary – see manufacturer's instructions. Heat the oil in a frying pan, add the onion and fry, stirring, for 5 minutes until pale golden. Add the beetroot to the pan with the drained beans, stock and plenty of salt and pepper. Bring to the boil, stirring.

2 Transfer the beetroot mixture to the slow cooker pot. Cover with the lid and cook on low for 3½–4½ hours until the beetroot is tender. Stir well and lift the pot out of the cooker.

3 Stir the diced cucumber into the yogurt and season with salt and pepper. Separate the lettuce leaves and rinse with cold water, drain well then arrange on 4 or 5 individual plates. Top with the warm beetroot salad, then add spoonfuls of the cucumber yogurt. Scatter sliced spring onions and coriander or mint over the top and serve at once.

Tip
• **Use dried beans instead of canned if you prefer – soak 200 g (7 oz) dried beans overnight, drain and rinse then boil rapidly in a saucepan of boiling water for 10 minutes before draining and using as above.**

Gingered chickpeas

Packed with protein, canned chickpeas are a healthy and economical storecupboard ingredient, used here to produce a supper dish ideally served with warmed pitta bread, plain rice or Coconut & Lime Rice (see page 181).

Serves 4

Preparation time: 15 minutes
Cooking time: 4–5 hours
Cooking temperature: low
Slow cooker size: standard

1 tablespoon olive oil
1 large onion, chopped
2 small parsnips, diced
2 carrots, diced
5 cm (2 inch) piece of fresh root ginger, finely chopped
1 teaspoon fennel seeds, roughly crushed
1 teaspoon turmeric
2 teaspoons paprika
400 g (13 oz) can chopped tomatoes
425 g (14 oz) can chickpeas, drained and rinsed
1 tablespoon soft light or dark brown sugar
600 ml (1 pint) hot vegetable stock
salt and pepper
torn coriander leaves, to garnish

1 Preheat the slow cooker if necessary – see manufacturer's instructions. Heat the oil in a frying pan, add the onion and fry, stirring, for 5 minutes until lightly browned. Add the diced parsnips and carrots and cook for 2–3 minutes.

2 Stir in the ginger, fennel seeds, turmeric and paprika then add the canned tomatoes, chickpeas, sugar and plenty of salt and pepper. Bring to the boil then transfer to the slow cooker pot. Stir in the hot stock.

3 Cover with the lid and cook on low for 4–5 hours until the vegetables are tender. Spoon into shallow dishes, garnish with torn coriander leaves and serve.

Tip
• **This dish freezes well in individual portions ready to be reheated in the microwave.**

Mushroom & cannellini bean stroganoff

Serves 4

Preparation time: 25 minutes
Cooking time: 2½–3 hours
Cooking temperature: low
Slow cooker size: standard

25 g (1 oz) dried porcini mushrooms
200 ml (7 fl oz) boiling water
25 g (1 oz) butter
1 tablespoon sunflower oil
1 large onion, chopped
3 celery sticks, sliced
250 g (8 oz) chestnut mushrooms, halved or
   quartered depending on size
1–2 garlic cloves, crushed or chopped (optional)
3 tablespoons plain flour
200 ml (7 fl oz) dry white wine or dry cider
150 ml (¼ pint) vegetable stock
2 teaspoons Dijon mustard
¼ teaspoon cayenne pepper
small bunch of thyme or a pinch of dried
410 g (13½ oz) can cannellini beans, drained and rinsed
salt
cayenne pepper or paprika, to garnish

1 Put the dried mushrooms in a bowl and cover with the boiling water. Leave to soak for 20 minutes. Meanwhile, preheat the slow cooker if required – see manufacturer's instructions.

2 Heat the butter and oil in a frying pan. Add the onion and fry until lightly browned. Stir in the celery, fresh mushrooms and garlic, if using, and cook for 2–3 minutes. Mix in the flour then gradually add the wine and stock. Stir in the mustard, cayenne pepper and a little salt. Reserve a couple of thyme sprigs to garnish then chop the rest and add to the pan together with the reconstituted dried mushrooms and their soaking liquid. Bring to the boil, stirring.

3 Pour the mushroom mixture into the slow cooker pot then stir in the beans. Cover with the lid and cook on low for 2½–3 hours. Spoon on to plates, sprinkle with thyme leaves stripped from the reserved sprigs and serve, topped with a sprinkling of cayenne pepper or paprika.

Cauliflower balti

This mild vegetarian curry is thickened towards the end of cooking with ground almonds. Serve it with warmed naan bread, which is delicious dunked in the sauce.

Serves 4

Preparation time: 25 minutes
Cooking time: 3¼–4¼ hours
Cooking temperature: high
Slow cooker size: standard

2 tablespoons sunflower oil
1 large onion, finely chopped
1 aubergine, diced
2 teaspoons cumin seeds, roughly crushed
2 teaspoons black mustard seeds
1 teaspoon turmeric
1 tablespoon mild curry paste
2–3 garlic cloves, chopped
400 g (13 oz) can chopped tomatoes
450 ml (¾ pint) vegetable stock
1 cauliflower, cut into medium-sized florets
1 baking potato, diced
3 tablespoons ground almonds
salt and pepper
torn coriander leaves, to garnish (optional)
naan bread, to serve

1 Preheat the slow cooker if necessary – see manufacturer's instructions. Heat the oil in a frying pan, add the onion and fry, stirring, for 5 minutes until lightly browned. Add the aubergine and fry for 3–4 minutes, until softened.

2 Stir in the spices, curry paste and garlic and cook for 1 minute. Add the canned tomatoes, stock and salt and pepper to taste and bring to the boil, stirring.

3 Put the cauliflower and potato in the slow cooker pot and add the tomato mixture. Cover with the lid and cook on high for 3–4 hours until the vegetables are cooked. Stir in the ground almonds and cook for 15 minutes more. Ladle into shallow dishes, garnish with torn coriander leaves, if using, and serve with warmed naan bread.

Chakchouka

Popular in North African countries, this ratatouille-style dish is finished by adding whole eggs towards the end of cooking so that they poach among the vegetables. Add some crushed dried chillies for a fiery kick, if you like your food hot.

Serves 4

Preparation time: 20 minutes
Cooking time: 3–4¼ hours
Cooking temperature: high
Slow cooker size: standard

2 tablespoons olive oil
1 large onion, roughly chopped
2 red peppers, cored, deseeded and chopped
1 orange pepper, cored, deseeded and chopped
2 large courgettes, coarsely chopped
2 garlic cloves, crushed
400 g (13 oz) can chopped tomatoes
2 teaspoons caster sugar
4 eggs
salt and pepper
crusty bread or garlic bread, to serve

1 Preheat the slow cooker if necessary – see manufacturer's instructions. Heat the oil in a frying pan, add the onion and fry, stirring, for 5 minutes until lightly browned. Add the peppers, courgettes and garlic and fry for 2 minutes. Stir in the canned tomatoes, sugar and salt and pepper to taste and bring to the boil.

2 Transfer the mixture to the slow cooker pot. Cover with the lid and cook on high for 3–4 hours. Stir the mixture then make 4 shallow indentations, slightly spaced apart, using a spoon. Crack an egg into each hollow, replace the lid of the slow cooker and cook on high for another 10–15 minutes until the egg whites are firm and the yolks still slightly soft. Spoon carefully on to serving plates and serve with warm crusty bread or garlic bread.

Tip
• **This dish freezes well, without the eggs, in individual portions ready to be reheated in the microwave.**

Split pea sofrito

This is like a Middle Eastern version of dhal, in which the split peas soften and thicken the sauce as they cook. It is served with toasted bread croutes topped with a fiery harissa-flavoured butter.

Serves 4

Preparation time: 30 minutes, plus overnight soaking
Cooking time: 6–7 hours
Cooking temperature: low
Slow cooker size: standard

150 g (5 oz) split peas, soaked overnight in cold water
3 tablespoons olive oil
1 large onion, chopped
3 carrots, diced
½ teaspoon *pimentón* (smoked paprika)
750 ml (1¼ pints) vegetable stock
salt and pepper

Topping
75 g (3 oz) butter
2 teaspoons harissa
2 garlic cloves, crushed
2 tablespoons chopped mint
1 small French stick, sliced

Tip
• **Harissa is a North African condiment made from chillies, garlic, dried coriander, mint and caraway seeds and widely available in large supermarkets. It is sold in small jars alongside the dry spices.**

1 Preheat the slow cooker if necessary – see manufacturer's instructions. Drain and rinse the soaked split peas. Heat the oil in a frying pan, add the onion and fry, stirring, for 5 minutes until lightly browned. Stir in the carrots and *pimentón* and cook for 1 minute.

2 Stir the split peas into the pan with the stock and season with salt and pepper. Bring to the boil, stirring, then cook for 2 minutes.

3 Pour the mixture into the slow cooker pot. Cover with the lid and cook on low for 6–7 hours. Meanwhile, make the spiced butter by beating the butter with the harissa in a shallow bowl. Mix in the garlic and mint, cover with clingfilm and chill until required.

4 Ladle the sofrito into shallow dishes and stir in a little of the spiced butter. Toast the slices of French bread and spread with the remaining spiced butter. Float the toasts on top of the sofrito and serve immediately.

& carrot cobbler

This dish smells so delicious when cooking that you may find you have a meat-eater at the table asking for a portion. If you are making it for strict vegetarians, check for a vegetarian symbol to make sure you select cheese made without rennet.

Serves 4

Preparation time: 45 minutes
Cooking time: 3–3½ hours
Cooking temperature: high
Slow cooker size: standard

1 tablespoon sunflower oil
1 large onion, chopped
500 g (1 lb) pumpkin or butternut squash, deseeded, peeled and diced
500 g (1 lb) carrots, diced
400 g (13 oz) can chopped tomatoes
250 ml (8 fl oz) vegetable stock
1 teaspoon caster sugar
2–3 rosemary sprigs or a pinch of dried
salt and pepper

Topping

150 g (5 oz) self-raising flour
pinch of salt
50 g (2 oz) butter
75 g (3 oz) blue cheese such as Stilton or Danish blue, rind removed, diced
4 teaspoons finely chopped rosemary (optional)
4 tablespoons water

1 Preheat the slow cooker if necessary – see manufacturer's instructions. Heat the oil in a frying pan, add the onion and fry, stirring, for 5 minutes until lightly browned.

2 Add the pumpkin, carrots, canned tomatoes, stock, sugar and rosemary and season with salt and pepper. Bring to the boil, stirring.

3 Transfer the vegetable mixture to the slow cooker pot. Cover with the lid and cook on high for 2½–3 hours until the vegetables are tender.

4 Meanwhile, make the topping. Put the flour and salt in a mixing bowl. Rub in the butter until the mixture resembles fine breadcrumbs. Mix in the cheese and rosemary, if using, then stir in enough of the water to make a smooth soft dough.

5 Pat the dough into a round 18 cm (7 inches) in diameter then cut into 8 segments. Arrange these on top of the pumpkin mixture. Replace the cooker lid and cook for another 30 minutes until the pastry is well risen and puffy. If the slow cooker pot fits under your grill, brown the topping under a preheated grill before serving.

Pistachio & apricot pilaf

This is a good storecupboard supper, quickly put together before you collect the kids from school, or ideal to start cooking before younger children's bath and story time, ready for an adults-only supper later.

Serves 4

Preparation time: 25 minutes
Cooking time: 2½–3 hours
Cooking temperature: low
Slow cooker size: standard

1 tablespoon olive oil
1 large onion, chopped
75 g (3 oz) mixed pistachios, walnuts and hazelnuts
25 g (1 oz) sunflower seeds
200 g (7 oz) easy-cook brown rice
1 litre (1¾ pints) vegetable stock
75 g (3 oz) ready-to-eat dried apricots, chopped
25 g (1 oz) currants
1 cinnamon stick, halved
6 cloves
3 bay leaves
1 tablespoon tomato purée
salt and pepper
lightly toasted mixed nuts, to garnish

1 Preheat the slow cooker if necessary – see manufacturer's instructions. Heat the oil in a frying pan, add the onion and fry, stirring, for 5 minutes until lightly browned.

2 Add the nuts and seeds and fry until lightly browned. Stir in the rice and stock, followed by the dried fruit, spices, bay leaves, tomato purée and season with salt and pepper to taste. Bring to the boil, stirring.

3 Transfer the mixture to the slow cooker pot. Cover with the lid and cook on low for 2½–3 hours until the rice is tender and the stock has been absorbed. Discard the cinnamon, cloves and bay leaves before serving, garnished with extra nuts.

Tip
• **To make in a larger slow cooker, increase the ingredient quantities by half as much again and cook for the same length of time.**

Sweet potato & chestnut jollof

Traditionally made with a rice base, this African-inspired dish has been made with pearl barley and flavoured with a little ground mace and whole cloves. It is topped with a coleslaw-style garnish.

Serves 4

Preparation time: 30 minutes
Cooking time: 4–5 hours
Cooking temperature: low
Slow cooker size: standard

1 tablespoon sunflower oil
1 large onion, chopped
½ teaspoon *pimentón* (smoked paprika)
  or chilli powder
500 g (1 lb) sweet potato, peeled and cut into
  chunks no larger than 1.5 cm (¾ inch)
240 g (7¾ oz) can whole peeled chestnuts, drained
100 g (3½ oz) pearl barley
¼ teaspoon ground mace
4 cloves
600 ml (1 pint) vegetable stock
1 tablespoon tomato purée
salt and pepper

To garnish
1 dessert apple, cored and finely chopped
1 small orange, segmented and chopped
125 g (4 oz) red or white cabbage, finely shredded
1 tablespoon finely chopped coriander

1 Preheat the slow cooker if necessary – see manufacturer's instructions. Heat the oil in a frying pan, add the onion and fry, stirring, for 5 minutes until lightly browned. Stir in the *pimentón* or chilli powder and cook for 1 minute.

2 Stir in the sweet potato, chestnuts, pearl barley, mace, cloves, stock, tomato purée and salt and pepper to taste and bring to the boil, stirring.

3 Transfer the mixture to the slow cooker pot. Cover with the lid and cook on low for 4–5 hours until the barley and potatoes are tender.

4 Combine the garnish ingredients. Spoon the jollof on to individual plates, top with the coleslaw mixture and serve.

Green bean risotto

with pesto

Risottos are incredibly easy to make in a slow cooker and because they cook so gently they are unlikely to boil dry. Frozen vegetables have been used to save time, but fresh ones could be used if preferred.

Serves 4

Preparation time: 20 minutes
Cooking time: 2 hours 5 minutes–2 hours 30 minutes
Cooking temperature: low
Slow cooker size: standard

25 g (1 oz) butter
1 tablespoon olive oil
1 onion, chopped
2 garlic cloves, chopped
250 g (8 oz) risotto rice
1.2 litres (2¼ pints) hot vegetable stock
2 teaspoons pesto
125 g (4 oz) extra fine frozen green beans
125 g (4 oz) frozen peas
salt and pepper

To garnish
Parmesan shavings
basil leaves

1 Preheat the slow cooker if necessary – see manufacturer's instructions. Heat the butter and oil in a saucepan, add the onion and fry, stirring, for 5 minutes until softened and just beginning to brown.

2 Stir in the garlic and rice and cook for 1 minute. Add all but 150 ml (¼ pint) of the stock, season with salt and pepper then bring to the boil. Transfer to the slow cooker pot, cover with the lid and cook on low for 1¾–2 hours.

3 Stir in the pesto and the remaining stock if some more liquid is needed. Place the frozen vegetables on top of the rice then replace the lid and cook for another 20–30 minutes until the vegetables are hot. Serve, garnished with Parmesan shavings and basil leaves.

Tip

- **If you need to avoid dairy produce, replace the butter with a little extra olive oil, use fresh basil leaves instead of the pesto and drizzle with lemon juice instead of finishing with Parmesan.**

These slow-cooked spicy beans get better the longer they are cooked. The stew is perfect for freezing in individual portions.

Serves 4–6

Preparation time: 30 minutes, plus overnight soaking
Cooking time: 8–10 hours
Cooking temperature: low
Slow cooker size: standard

250 g (8 oz) dried black beans, soaked overnight in cold water
2 tablespoons olive oil
1 large onion, chopped
2 carrots, diced
2 celery sticks, sliced
2–3 garlic cloves, chopped
1 teaspoon fennel seeds, crushed
1 teaspoon cumin seeds, crushed
2 teaspoons coriander seeds, crushed
1 teaspoon chilli powder or *pimentón* (smoked paprika)
400 g (13 oz) can chopped tomatoes
300 ml (½ pint) vegetable stock
1 tablespoon brown sugar
salt and pepper

Avocado salsa
1 avocado
grated rind and juice of 1 lime
½ red onion, finely chopped
2 tomatoes, diced
2 tablespoons chopped coriander leaves

To serve
boiled rice or crusty bread

1 Preheat the slow cooker if necessary – see manufacturer's instructions. Drain and rinse the soaked beans. Place in a saucepan, add fresh water to cover and bring to the boil. Boil vigorously for 10 minutes, then drain into a sieve.

2 Meanwhile, heat the oil in the saucepan, add the onion and fry, stirring, for 5 minutes until softened. Add the carrots, celery and garlic and fry for 2–3 minutes. Stir the crushed fennel and cumin seeds into the vegetables with the chilli powder or *pimentón* and cook for 1 minute.

3 Add the canned tomatoes, stock, sugar and a little pepper. Bring to the boil then pour into the slow cooker pot. Mix in the beans, press under the liquid, then cover the pot and cook on low for 8–10 hours.

4 About 10 minutes before serving, make the avocado salsa: halve the avocado, remove the stone and peel away the skin. Dice the flesh, toss with the lime rind and juice then mix with the onion, tomatoes and coriander.

5 Season the cooked beans to taste with salt then serve with boiled rice or crusty bread, accompanied by the avocado salsa.

black bean stew

Dum aloo

For a healthy, meat-free supper serve this spiced new potato and spinach curry with a lentil dhal and plain rice or hot naan bread.

Serves 4

Preparation time: 15 minutes
Cooking time: 6¼–7¼ hours
Cooking temperature: high
Slow cooker size: standard

2 tablespoons sunflower oil
1 large onion, sliced
1 teaspoon cumin seeds, crushed
4 cardamom pods, crushed
1 teaspoon black onion seeds (optional)
1 teaspoon ground turmeric
½ teaspoon ground cinnamon
2.5 cm (1 inch) fresh root ginger, peeled and finely
  chopped
400 g (13 oz) can chopped tomatoes
300 ml (½ pint) vegetable stock
1 teaspoon caster sugar
750 g (1½ lb) baby new potatoes
100 g (3½ oz) baby leaf spinach
salt and pepper
coriander leaves, to garnish

1 Preheat the slow cooker if necessary – see manufacturer's instructions. Heat the oil in a large frying pan, add the onion and fry, stirring, for 5 minutes or until lightly browned.

2 Mix in the cumin seeds, cardamom pods and seeds, onion seeds, if using, ground spices and ginger. Cook for 1 minute, then mix in the tomatoes, stock, sugar and season with salt and pepper. Bring to the boil, stirring.

3 Cut the potatoes into thick slices or halves (if they are small) so that all the pieces are of a similar size. Transfer to the slow cooker pot and pour the sauce over the top.

4 Cover and cook on high for 6–7 hours or until the potatoes are tender. Add the spinach and cook on high for 15 minutes more until it is just wilted. Stir the curry and serve sprinkled with torn coriander leaves.

Tip
• **If you like curries on the hot side, add a fresh chopped red chilli or some dried chilli powder at step 2.**

Red Thai pumpkin curry

Cubes of golden butternut squash, baby new potatoes and carrots are simmered in a creamy coconut milk sauce lightly spiced with Thai curry paste, garlic and soy sauce to make this hearty meal.

Serves 4

Preparation time: 25 minutes
Cooking time: 7–8 hours
Cooking temperature: low
Slow cooker size: standard

1 tablespoon sunflower oil
1 onion, chopped
4 teaspoons red Thai curry paste
2 garlic cloves, finely chopped
400 ml (14 fl oz) can coconut milk
300 ml (½ pint) vegetable stock
1 tablespoon Thai fish sauce (optional)
1 tablespoon soy sauce
1 butternut squash, about 700 g (1 lb 7 oz), peeled, deseeded and cut into chunks
250 g (8 oz) baby new potatoes, thickly sliced
250 g (8 oz) carrots, thinly sliced
sprigs of coriander or basil (optional)
125 g (4 oz) medium rice noodles

1 Preheat the slow cooker if necessary – see manufacturer's instructions. Heat the oil in a large frying pan, add the onion and fry, stirring, for 5 minutes or until lightly browned. Mix in the curry paste and garlic and cook for 1 minute. Stir in the coconut milk, stock, fish sauce, if using, and soy sauce. Bring to the boil, stirring.

2 Put the butternut squash, potatoes and carrots into the slow cooker pot. Pour over the sauce, press the vegetables down into the liquid, cover and cook on low for 7–8 hours or until all the vegetables are tender. Just before the end of cooking, add the herbs to the slow cooker pot, if using, and stir through.

3 Put the noodles in a shallow bowl, cover with boiling water and leave to soak for 4–5 minutes or cook according to the packet instructions.

4 Drain the noodles, divide between bowls and spoon the curry over the top to serve.

Tips
- **Make sure that all the pieces of potato are the same size so that they are all cooked through evenly.**
- **Do not add fish sauce if you are serving this dish to vegetarians.**

vegetable stew

The number seven is thought to be lucky in Moroccan culture, and this dish is a good way of encouraging your family to boost its intake of healthy vegetables.

Serves 4

Preparation time: 25 minutes
Cooking time: 6 hours 15 minutes–8 hours 20 minutes
Cooking temperature: low and high
Slow cooker size: standard

2 tablespoons olive oil
1 large onion, chopped
2 carrots
300 g (10 oz) swede
1 red pepper, cored, deseeded and chopped
3 garlic cloves, finely chopped
200 g (7 oz) frozen broad beans
400 g (13 oz) can chopped tomatoes
3 teaspoons harissa (chilli paste)
1 teaspoon ground turmeric
2 cm (¾ inch) fresh root ginger, peeled and
  finely chopped
250 ml (8 fl oz) vegetable stock
125 g (4 oz) okra, thickly sliced
salt and pepper
mint leaves, to garnish (optional)
couscous, to serve

1 Preheat the slow cooker if necessary – see manufacturer's instructions. Heat the oil in a large frying pan, add the onion and fry, stirring, for 5 minutes or until lightly browned.

2 Stir in the carrots, swede, red pepper, garlic, broad beans and tomatoes. Mix in the harissa, turmeric and ginger, then pour on the stock and season with salt and pepper. Bring to the boil, stirring.

3 Spoon the mixture into the slow cooker pot and press the vegetables beneath the surface of the stock. Cover and cook on low for 6–8 hours or until the root vegetables are tender.

4 Stir in the okra, cover and cook on high for 15–20 minutes or until the okra are tender but still bright green. Garnish with torn mint leaves, if using, and serve with couscous soaked in boiling water and flavoured with olive oil, lemon juice and sultanas.

Tips

- **Harissa, a paste made from chillies, oil, garlic and coriander, is widely available in supermarkets.**
- **Cut the carrot and swede into pieces that are the same size so that they will be cooked through evenly.**

141

Spiced date pilaf

This rice dish makes a great main course for vegetarians. Alternatively, serve it as an accompaniment to roasted chicken or barbecued chicken kebabs.

Serves 4

Preparation time: 15 minutes
Cooking time: 2–2¼ hours
Cooking temperature: low
Slow cooker size: standard

50 g (2 oz) butter
1 onion, finely chopped
2 garlic cloves, finely chopped
1 cinnamon stick, halved
6 cardamom pods, crushed
4 whole cloves
1 bay leaf
1 teaspoon ground turmeric
250 g (8 oz) easy-cook, long-grain brown rice
750 ml (1¼ pints) hot vegetable stock
50 g (2 oz) stoned dates, chopped
50 g (2 oz) raisins
salt and pepper

1 Preheat the slow cooker if necessary – see manufacturer's instructions. Heat the butter in a frying pan, add the onion and fry gently, stirring, for 5 minutes or until softened.

2 Stir in the garlic, cinnamon, cardamom pods and seeds, cloves and bay leaf. Cook for 1 minute, then mix in the turmeric and rice and cook for 1 more minute.

3 Transfer the mixture to the slow cooker pot, pour in the hot stock, then add the dried fruits and season with salt and pepper. Stir together and cover.

4 Cook the pilaf on low for 2–2¼ hours or until the rice is tender and has absorbed nearly all the stock. Stir and spoon on to plates.

Winter vegetable ragout with lager

Serves 4

Preparation time: 30 minutes
Cooking time: 9¼–10¼ hours
Cooking temperature: low and high
Slow cooker size: standard

40 g (1½ oz) butter
1 tablespoon sunflower oil
200 g (7 oz) shallots, halved
1 leek, thinly sliced (keep white and green slices
    separate)
25 g (1 oz) plain flour
325 ml (11 fl oz) lager
300 ml (½ pint) vegetable stock
3 teaspoons wholegrain mustard
375 g (12 oz) swede, cut into 2 cm (¾ inch) dice
375 g (12 oz) parsnips, cut into 2 cm (¾ inch) dice
375 g (12 oz) carrots, cut into 2 cm (¾ inch) dice
1 sheet ready-rolled puff pastry, about 200 g (7 oz),
    thawed if frozen
beaten egg, to glaze
100 g (3½ oz) strong Cheddar cheese, grated
salt and pepper

1 Preheat the slow cooker if necessary – see manufacturer's instructions. Heat 15 g (½ oz) butter and oil in a large frying pan, add the shallots and white leek slices and fry until lightly browned. Scoop the onions and leeks out of the pan with a slotted spoon and transfer to a plate.

2 Melt the remaining butter and stir in the flour. Gradually mix in the lager and stock. Stir in the mustard, season with salt and peper and bring to the boil, stirring.

3 Put the root vegetables into the slow cooker pot. Add the fried shallots and leeks and pour the lager sauce over the top. Press the vegetables beneath the surface of the liquid, cover and cook on low for 9–10 hours.

4 Unroll the pastry, cut it into quarters and transfer to an oiled baking sheet. Brush with the egg and sprinkle with a little of the cheese. Bake in a preheated oven, 200°C (400°F), Gas Mark 6, for 12–15 minutes or until well risen and golden. Stir the remaining cheese and green leek slices into the slow cooker pot. Cook on high for 15 minutes.

5 Spoon the vegetables into bowls and top each with a puff pastry lid.

Mixed beans with

This garlicky, ruby-red vegetarian feast is topped with French bread toast, crumbled feta cheese and rosemary.

Serves 4

Preparation time: 20 minutes
Cooking time: 6–8 hours
Cooking temperature: low
Slow cooker size: standard

1 tablespoon olive oil
1 onion, chopped
5 small raw beetroot, about 500 g (1 lb), trimmed, peeled and cut into 1 cm (½ inch) cubes
2 carrots, about 200 g (7 oz), diced
2 garlic cloves, finely chopped
450 ml (¾ pint) vegetable or chicken stock
200 g (7 oz) red cabbage, shredded and woody core discarded
410 g (13¼ oz) can mixed beans, drained
1 bay leaf
2 tablespoons red wine vinegar
1 tablespoon caster sugar
salt and pepper

Topping

12 thin slices of French stick
150 g (5 oz) feta cheese, drained
1 tablespoon finely chopped rosemary leaves
2 tablespoons olive oil

1 Preheat the slow cooker if necessary – see manufacturer's instructions. Heat the oil in a large frying pan, add the onion and fry, stirring, for 5 minutes or until lightly browned. Stir in the beetroot, carrots and garlic and cook for 3 minutes. Pour in the stock and bring to the boil.

2 Transfer the beetroot mixture to the slow cooker pot. Add the red cabbage, drained beans, bay leaf and season to taste with salt and pepper. Press the vegetables beneath the surface of the liquid, cover and cook on low for 6–8 hours or until the beetroot is cooked.

3 Stir in the vinegar and sugar and replace the lid. Continue cooking until ready to serve.

4 Meanwhile, make the toasts. Put the bread slices under the grill until lightly browned on both sides. Crumble the cheese on top, sprinkle with rosemary and a little black pepper and press them down on the toast with the back of a fork. Drizzle with the oil and grill for a few more minutes or until hot. Arrange the toasts on top of the beetroot mixture, lift the pot from the slow cooker and transfer it to the table to serve.

Tip
• Garlic and herb cream cheese or crumbled Stilton would make delicious alternative toppings for the toast.

feta & rosemary toasts

Mixed mushroom

This hearty vegetarian main course is made with three types of mushroom simmered with Puy lentils in a tomato sauce. Serve with soft, buttery polenta and a rocket salad.

Serves 4

Preparation time: 25 minutes
Cooking time: 6–8 hours
Cooking temperature: low
Slow cooker size: standard

2 tablespoons olive oil, plus extra to serve
1 large onion, chopped
3 garlic cloves, finely chopped
400 g (13 oz) can chopped tomatoes
300 ml (½ pint) vegetable stock
150 ml (¼ pint) red wine (or extra stock)
1 tablespoon tomato purée
2 teaspoons caster sugar
125 g (4 oz) Puy lentils
375 g (12 oz) cup mushrooms, halved or
    quartered depending on size
125 g (4 oz) shiitake mushrooms, halved if large
4 large field mushrooms, about 250 g (8 oz), whole
salt and pepper
fried polenta, to serve

To garnish
rocket leaves
Parmesan cheese shavings

1 Preheat the slow cooker if necessary – see manufacturer's instructions. Heat the oil in a large frying pan, add the onion and fry, stirring, for 5 minutes or until lightly browned. Mix in the garlic, tomatoes, stock, wine, if using, tomato purée, sugar and season with salt and pepper. Add the Puy lentils and bring to the boil.

2 Put the mushrooms in the slow cooker pot, pour over the lentil mixture, cover and cook on low for 6–8 hours, stirring once if possible.

3 Garnish with rocket leaves tossed with Parmesan shavings and a drizzle of olive oil and serve with fried rounds of polenta.

Tip
• **The mushrooms will completely fill the slow cooker when you first add them, but as they cook they will lose their bulk and simmer gently in the sauce.**

Mediterranean fennel

A ratatouille-style dish made with Florence fennel, peppers and carrots, gently cooked in a rich garlicky sauce, then sprinkled with a buttery croûton and mixed nut topping.

Serves 4

Preparation time: 30 minutes
Cooking time: 6–7 hours
Cooking temperature: high
Slow cooker size: standard

1 tablespoon olive oil
1 large onion, chopped
2 garlic cloves, finely chopped
2 tablespoons plain flour
400 g (13 oz) can chopped tomatoes
300 ml (½ pint) vegetable stock
1 teaspoon light muscovado sugar
2 fennel bulbs, cut into small chunks
2 peppers (orange and red), cored, deseeded and chopped
2 carrots, cut into small dice
salt and pepper
green salad, to serve

Topping

100 g (3½ oz) ciabatta or rustic bread
3 tablespoons olive oil
25 g (1 oz) butter
2 garlic cloves, finely chopped
2 tablespoons pumpkin seeds (optional)
75 g (3 oz) almonds or hazelnuts, roughly chopped

1 Preheat the slow cooker if necessary – see manufacturer's instructions. Heat the oil in a large frying pan, add the onion and fry, stirring, for 5 minutes or until lightly browned. Add the garlic and cook for 2 minutes.

2 Stir in the flour, then add the tomatoes, stock and sugar. Season to taste with salt and pepper and bring to the boil, stirring.

3 Put all the chopped vegetables in the slow cooker pot, pour the hot tomato mixture over the top and press the vegetables below the surface of the sauce. Cover and cook on high for 6–7 hours or until the vegetables are tender.

4 Just before you are ready to serve, tear the bread for the topping into small pieces. Heat the oil and butter in a clean frying pan, add the bread, garlic, pumpkin seeds, if using, and nuts and fry over a moderate heat, stirring until golden.

5 Spoon the fennel mixture into shallow bowls and sprinkle the croûton crumble on top. Serve with a green salad.

with nutty crumble

Feta tiganito

Fried layers of garlicky sliced aubergine, peppers and a rich tomato sauce are topped with melting feta cheese. Serve with warm pitta breads and salad.

Serves 4–5

Preparation time: 30 minutes
Cooking time: 5–6 hours
Cooking temperature: high
Slow cooker size: standard

2 large aubergines, thickly sliced
4–5 tablespoons olive oil
2 onions, roughly chopped
3 garlic cloves, finely chopped
2 × 400 g (13 oz) cans chopped tomatoes
2 teaspoons caster sugar
large pinch of grated nutmeg
small bunch of oregano or basil
2 peppers (red and orange), cored, deseeded
  and diced
150 g (5 oz) feta cheese, drained and crumbled
40 g (1½ oz) pitted black olives
salt and pepper

To serve
toasted pitta bread
green salad

1 Preheat the slow cooker if necessary – see manufacturer's instructions. Lay the aubergine slices on a tray, sprinkle with salt and set aside for 15–20 minutes or until the juices begin to run.

2 Heat 1 tablespoon oil of in a saucepan, add the onions and fry until just beginning to brown. Add the garlic, fry for 1 minute, then mix in the tomatoes, sugar and nutmeg. Season to taste with salt and pepper. Tear half the herbs into small pieces and add them to the sauce.

3 Rinse the aubergine slices under cold water to remove the salt, drain them well and dry with kitchen paper. Heat a little of the remaining oil in a large frying pan and fry the aubergine slices in batches, adding more oil as needed, until browned on both sides. Transfer to a plate.

4 Layer the aubergines, peppers, feta and hot sauce alternately in the slow cooker pot, finishing with a thick layer of sauce and feta. Sprinkle the olives on top, cover and cook on high for 5–6 hours. Spoon into shallow bowls, garnish with the remaining herb leaves and serve with toasted pitta bread and a green salad.

Mixed vegetable bourride

Saffron adds a delicate flavour to this Mediterranean mix of peppers, plum tomatoes, courgettes and cannellini beans. Serve in shallow soup bowls topped with toasted French bread and rouille and eat with forks and spoons to scoop up the garlicky sauce.

Serves 4
Preparation time: 30 minutes
Cooking time: 6½–8¾ hours
Cooking temperature: low and high
Slow cooker size: standard

1 tablespoon olive oil
1 large red onion, roughly chopped
3 peppers (red, yellow and orange), cored, deseeded and diced
2–3 garlic cloves, finely chopped
500 g (1 lb) plum tomatoes, peeled if liked, diced
410 g (13½ oz) can cannellini beans, drained
150 ml (¼ pint) dry white wine
150 ml (¼ pint) vegetable stock
2 large pinches of saffron threads
2 teaspoons caster sugar
400 g (13 oz) courgettes, cubed
salt and pepper

To serve
1 red chilli, halved, deseeded and finely chopped
2 garlic cloves, finely chopped
4 tablespoons mayonnaise
½ French stick, sliced

1 Preheat the slow cooker if necessary – see manufacturer's instructions. Heat the oil in a large frying pan, add the onion and fry, stirring, for 5 minutes or until lightly browned. Add the peppers and garlic and fry for 2 minutes.

2 Mix in the tomatoes, beans, wine, stock, saffron and sugar. Season to taste with salt and pepper, then bring to the boil and spoon into the slow cooker pot. Press the vegetables beneath the liquid, cover and cook on low for 6–8 hours or until the vegetables are tender.

3 Stir the courgettes into the slow cooker pot and cook on high for 30–45 minutes or until they are just tender but still bright green.

4 Meanwhile, mix the chilli and garlic into the mayonnaise. Toast the bread just before serving. Ladle the bourride into shallow soup bowls, top with the toast and spoon a little rouille on to each slice.

Tip
• Rouille is a reddish, chilli-based sauce from the south of France, which is traditionally served with fish stews but is also delicious with vegetables.

153

Rosemary pudding with

mushrooms & chestnuts

Serves 4

Preparation time: 45 minutes
Cooking time: 5–6 hours
Cooking temperature: high
Slow cooker size: standard

Sauce

15 g (½ oz) butter
1 tablespoon sunflower oil
1 onion, thinly sliced
1 tablespoon plain flour
300 ml (½ pint) vegetable stock
5 tablespoons ruby port
1 teaspoon Dijon mustard
1 teaspoon tomato purée
salt and pepper

Pastry

300 g (10 oz) self-raising flour
½ teaspoon salt
150 g (5 oz) shredded vegetable suet
2 tablespoons finely chopped rosemary leaves
about 200 ml (7 fl oz) cold water

Filling

1 large flat mushroom, sliced
125 g (4 oz) chestnut cup mushrooms, sliced
200 g (7 oz) vacuum pack whole peeled chestnuts

1 Preheat the slow cooker if necessary – see manufacturer's instructions. Make the sauce. Heat the butter and oil in a large frying pan, add the onion and fry for 5 minutes. Stir in the flour, then mix in the stock, port, mustard and tomato purée. Add salt and pepper, bring to the boil, stirring, then take off the heat.

2 Make the pastry. Mix together the flour, salt, suet and rosemary. Gradually add enough cold water to mix to a soft but not sticky dough. Knead lightly, then roll out to a circle 33 cm (13 inches) across.

3 Cut a one-quarter segment from the circle of pastry and reserve. Lift the remaining pastry into an oiled 1.25 litre (2¼ pint) pudding basin and bring the cut edges together, overlapping them slightly so that the basin is completely lined with pastry, then press them together to seal. Layer the sauce, mushrooms and chestnuts into the basin, finishing with the sauce.

4 Pat the reserved pastry into a circle the same size as the top of the basin. Dampen the edges of the pastry in the basin with a little water and press the lid in place. Cover with buttered foil and dome the foil slightly. Tie in place with string, then lower into the slow cooker pot with a string handle (see page 15).

5 Pour boiling water into the slow cooker pot so that it comes halfway up the sides of the basin. Cover and cook on high for 5–6 hours.

Fish & seafood

Squid

in red wine

This squid, cooked slowly in the traditional Greek way with red wine and bay leaves, seems to almost melt in the mouth. Serve as a light lunch for four or as a starter for six people.

Serves 4–6

Preparation time: 25 minutes
Cooking time: 3½–4½ hours
Cooking temperature: low
Slow cooker size: standard

625 g (1¼ lb) prepared squid, defrosted if frozen
2 tablespoons olive oil
2 large onions, thinly sliced
375 g (12 oz) plum tomatoes, skinned if liked and
   roughly chopped
2–3 garlic cloves, chopped
2 bay leaves
2–3 rosemary sprigs
200 ml (7 fl oz) red wine
2 tablespoons red or white wine vinegar
2 teaspoons sugar
salt and pepper
crusty bread, to serve

1 Preheat the slow cooker if necessary – see manufacturer's instructions. Rinse the squid in plenty of cold water. Drain well, pull out the tentacles, put in a separate bowl, cover and return to the refrigerator. Cut the body of the squid into 1 cm (½ inch) thick slices then set aside.

2 Heat the oil in a frying pan, add the onions and fry, stirring, for 5 minutes until lightly browned. Add the tomatoes and garlic and cook for 2–3 minutes then add the bay leaves, rosemary, wine, vinegar, sugar and plenty of salt and pepper.

3 Stir the sliced squid into the tomato mixture and bring to the boil. Transfer to the slow cooker pot, press the squid below the level of the liquid then cover with the lid and cook on low for 3–4 hours.

4 Stir well, add the reserved squid tentacles and cook for 30 minutes more. Spoon the squid into shallow dishes and serve with plenty of warm crusty bread to mop up the sauce.

Tips

• **To make in a larger slow cooker, increase the ingredient quantities by half as much again and cook for the same amount of time.**

• **One medium octopus can be used in place of the squid but simmer in a saucepan of water for 1 hour before slicing and continuing with the recipe as above.**

Stuffed monkfish
with coriander & chilli

This meaty, lobster-like white fish is stuffed with a wonderfully refreshing mix of coriander, chilli and lime rind and cooked with pak choi.

Serves 3–4

Preparation time: 40 minutes
Cooking time: about 2½ hours
Cooking temperature: low
Slow cooker size: standard

1 monkfish tail, about 875 g (1¾ lb)
small bunch of coriander
50 g (2 oz) butter
grated rind and juice of 1 lime
1–2 large mild red chillies, halved, deseeded and
    finely chopped
2 spring onions, thinly sliced
150 ml (¼ pint) hot fish stock
150 g (5 oz) pak choi, thickly sliced
salt and pepper
lime wedges, to garnish
white rice or soft noodles, to serve

1 Preheat the slow cooker if necessary – see manufacturer's instructions. Check that all the skin and thin membrane under the skin has been removed from the fish. Cut a slit along the length of the piece of fish and remove the central bone and attached fins.

2 Roughly chop 40 g (1½ oz) of the coriander leaves and beat into the butter with the lime rind, chopped chillies and spring onions. Spoon the mixture into the cavity of the fish and tie the fish neatly at intervals with fine string.

3 Arrange the fish in the slow cooker pot, bending it if necessary to fit. Season with salt and pepper and pour the stock around the fish. Cover with the lid and cook on low for 1½ hours. Turn the fish over and cook for 30–45 minutes more until it is opaque and flakes when pressed with a knife.

4 Add the pak choi to the slow cooker and press into the stock. Replace the lid and cook for another 15–25 minutes until just tender. Carefully transfer the fish to a shallow serving dish and remove the string. Drizzle with the lime juice and garnish with the remaining coriander. Spoon the pak choi around the fish and pour the remaining sauce into a separate bowl. Garnish with lime wedges and serve with white rice or soft noodles.

Crystal steamed trout

Part-steaming, part-baking, slow cooking brings out the flavour of these whole cooked trout and intensifies the flavour of the Chinese-style vegetable topping. You need an oval-shaped cooker for this recipe so as to fit in the trout snugly, side by side.

Serves 4

Preparation time: 30 minutes
Cooking time: 1¼–1½ hours
Cooking temperature: high
Slow cooker size: extra large

4 small trout, about 1 kg (2 lb),
  gutted and heads removed
3.5 cm (1½ inch) piece of fresh root ginger, peeled
1 carrot
4 spring onions
½ red pepper, cored and deseeded
grated rind and juice of 1 lime
2 teaspoons sunflower oil
3 tablespoons sesame seeds
1 tablespoon soy sauce
2 limes, halved, to serve
egg-fried rice, to serve

1 Preheat the slow cooker if necessary – see manufacturer's instructions. Stand a plate on an upturned individual tart tin or a biscuit cutter at the bottom of your slow cooker pot. Pour enough boiling water into the pot to come just below the plate.

2 Rinse the trout and lay them side by side on a large piece of buttered foil. Cut the ginger, carrot, spring onions and red pepper into thin strips. Tuck a few strips inside the trout cavities and sprinkle the rest over the top. Spoon the lime rind and juice over the trout.

3 Heat the oil in a frying pan, add the sesame seeds and cook for 2–3 minutes until browned. Remove from the heat, stir in the soy sauce then spoon over the trout.

4 Fold the foil up and over the trout and seal the edges together well. Then carefully lower the foil parcel on to the plate in the slow cooker pot. Cover with the lid and cook on high for 1¼–1½ hours. To check that the fish is done, lift the foil parcel out of the cooker. Open it out and press a knife into the inside of the trout – the flesh should flake easily when pressed.

5 Lift the trout out of the foil and transfer the foil parcel to a large serving plate. Serve with halved limes, to squeeze over the trout, and egg-fried rice.

161

Italian

Large moist flakes of white fish, chunky pieces of mixed seafood and tiny pasta shapes make this tangy lemon and tomato-based stew a hearty family meal in a bowl.

Serves 4

Preparation time: 30 minutes
Cooking time: 2 hours 20 minutes–3 hours 30 minutes
Cooking temperature: low and high
Slow cooker size: standard

1 tablespoon olive oil
1 large onion, chopped
2 garlic cloves, chopped
400 g (13 oz) can chopped tomatoes
grated rind and juice of 1 lemon
450 ml (¾ pint) fish stock
1 tablespoon tomato purée
2 teaspoons caster sugar
500 g (1 lb) pollack, haddock or hake, skinned and
    cut into large chunks
1 red pepper, cored, deseeded and diced
100 g (3½ oz) small pasta shells or macaroni
1 courgette, finely diced
100 g (3½ oz) frozen cooked peeled prawns,
    defrosted and rinsed (optional)
salt and pepper
basil leaves or pesto, to garnish
ciabatta or garlic bread, to serve

1 Preheat the slow cooker if necessary – see manufacturer's instructions. Heat the oil in a frying pan, add the onion and fry, stirring, for 5 minutes until lightly browned. Add the garlic then the canned tomatoes, lemon rind and juice, stock, tomato purée, sugar and salt and pepper. Bring to the boil, stirring.

2 Place the fish in the slow cooker pot, add the pepper and pasta, then cover with the tomato sauce. Cover with the lid and cook on low for 2–3 hours until the fish and pasta are tender.

3 Turn the cooker setting to high. Stir in the courgette and prawns, if using, and cook for 20–30 minutes until piping hot and the courgette is tender. Spoon into shallow dishes, sprinkle with basil leaves or spoonfuls of pesto and serve with warmed ciabatta or garlic bread.

seafood casserole

Swordfish bourride

Serves 4

Preparation time: 30 minutes
Cooking time: 1 hour 20 minutes–2 hours
Cooking temperature: low and high
Slow cooker size: standard

2 tablespoons olive oil

1 large onion, chopped

2–3 garlic cloves, crushed

1 teaspoon paprika

large pinch of fresh saffron

3 plum tomatoes, skinned and chopped

4 tablespoons white wine

1 tablespoon tomato purée

2 teaspoons caster sugar

2 large swordfish or tuna steaks, about
   625 g (1 1/4 lb), halved

200 g (7 oz) cooked mixed seafood – to include
   prawns, mussels and squid, defrosted if frozen
   and rinsed

salt and pepper

To garnish

rouille (optional)

green salad

French bread

1 Preheat the slow cooker if necessary – see manufacturer's instructions. Heat the oil in a frying pan, add the onion and fry, stirring, for 5 minutes until lightly browned. Stir in the garlic and paprika and cook for 1 minute.

2 Add the saffron, tomatoes, wine, tomato purée, sugar and salt and pepper and bring it to the boil, stirring.

3 Arrange the fish steaks in the slow cooker pot and pour the sauce over the top. Cover with the lid and cook on low for 1–1 1/2 hours until the fish is cooked through.

4 Turn the cooker setting to high and stir in the seafood, cook for 20–30 minutes more until piping hot. Spoon on to serving plates and serve topped with spoonfuls of rouille (mayonnaise mixed with finely chopped red chilli and garlic) if liked, green salad and warmed French bread.

Tip

• **Don't be tempted to add extra liquid – it's surprising how much liquid there will be by the end of cooking.**

Poached salmon
with beurre blanc

Serves 4

Preparation time: 25 minutes
Cooking time: 1½–1¾ hours
Cooking temperature: low
Slow cooker size: standard

100 g (3½ oz) butter
1 large onion, thinly sliced
1 lemon, sliced
500 g (1 lb) piece of thick-end salmon fillet, no
    longer than 18 cm (7 inches)
1 bay leaf
200 ml (7 fl oz) dry white wine
150 ml (¼ pint) fish stock
3 tablespoons finely chopped chives,
    plus extra to garnish
salt and pepper
lemon slices, to garnish
new potatoes and a green salad, to serve

1 Preheat the slow cooker if necessary – see manufacturer's instructions. Brush inside the slow cooker pot with a little of the butter. Fold a large piece of foil into 3 then place at the bottom of the pot with the ends sticking up to use as a strap. Arrange the onion slices and half of the lemon slices over the foil.

2 Place the salmon, flesh side uppermost, on top. Season with salt and pepper then add the bay leaf and remaining lemon slices. Pour the wine and stock into a saucepan, bring to the boil then pour over the salmon. Put the lid on, then cook on low for 1½–1¾ hours until the fish is opaque and flakes easily when pressed with a knife.

3 Lift the salmon carefully out of the pot using the foil strap, draining off as much liquid as possible. Place on a serving plate, discard the bay leaf, lemon and onion slices, and keep warm. Strain the cooking liquid into a saucepan and boil rapidly for 4–5 minutes until reduced to about 4 tablespoons.

4 Reduce the heat and gradually whisk in small pieces of the remaining butter, little by little, until the sauce thickens and becomes creamy. (Don't be tempted to hurry making the sauce either by adding the butter in one go, or by increasing the heat to the sauce or you may find that it separates.) Stir in the chopped chives and adjust the seasoning if needed.

5 Cut the salmon into 4 portions, discard the skin and transfer to individual plates. Spoon a little of the sauce around the fish. Garnish with lemon slices and whole chives. Serve with new potatoes and a green salad.

Pesto baked salmon

The gentle cooking that takes place in a slow cooker means that the fish stays moist and there is no danger that it will break up. Serve the salmon with rice mixed with lots of chopped basil and parsley or with baby new potatoes.

Serves 4
Preparation time: 20 minutes
Cooking time: 3–3½ hours
Cooking temperature: low
Slow cooker size: standard

500 g (1 lb) thick-end salmon fillet
2 teaspoons pesto
1 red pepper, cored, deseeded and chopped
250 g (8 oz) cherry tomatoes, halved
4 spring onions, thinly sliced
200 ml (7 fl oz) dry white wine
150 ml (¼ pint) fish stock
salt and pepper
basil leaves, to garnish

1 Preheat the slow cooker if necessary – see manufacturer's instructions. Take a long piece of foil and fold it in half widthways. Place the salmon on the centre of the foil and spread the top with the pesto.

2 Holding the ends of the foil, lower the salmon into the slow cooker pot (see page 13). Add the red pepper, tomatoes and spring onions. Pour the wine and stock into a frying pan, season to taste with salt and pepper and bring to the boil. Pour the liquid into the slow cooker. Fold the ends of the foil down if necessary so that they fit inside the slow cooker, then cover and cook on low for 3–3½ hours or until the fish flakes into opaque pieces and the vegetables are just tender.

3 Spoon the vegetables on to plates. Use the foil strap to lift the salmon from the pot and cut it into 4 pieces. Arrange these next to the vegetables. Pour the stock into a frying pan and boil rapidly for 2–3 minutes or until it is reduced by half. Pour the sauce over the salmon and serve garnished with basil leaves.

Saffron & wild

Meaty cod loins are cooked above a delicately perfumed mix of risotto and black wild rice grains to make a relaxed supper dish that is perfect to share with friends.

Serves 4

Preparation time: 25 minutes
Cooking time: 1¾–2 hours
Cooking temperature: low
Slow cooker size: standard

25 g (1 oz) butter
1 tablespoon olive oil
1 onion, chopped
2 garlic cloves, finely chopped
40 g (1½ oz) wild rice
250 g (8 oz) risotto rice
2 large pinches of saffron
grated rind of 1 lemon
1.2 litres (2 pints) hot fish or vegetable stock
2 large cod loins, about 500 g (1 lb) in total
salt and pepper
basil leaves, to garnish

1 Preheat the slow cooker if necessary – see manufacturer's instructions. Heat the butter and oil in a large frying pan, add the onion and fry gently for 5 minutes or until softened but not coloured. Stir in the garlic and cook for 2 minutes.

2 Stir in the wild rice, risotto rice, saffron and lemon rind. Add the stock and bring to the boil.

3 Pour the rice mixture into the slow cooker pot, season to taste with salt and pepper and add the cod, pressing the fish just beneath the surface of the stock. Cover and cook on low for 1¾–2 hours or until the rice is cooked and has absorbed most of the stock.

4 Break each cod loin in half, spoon the rice and fish into shallow bowls or plates, sprinkle with basil leaves and serve immediately.

Tips

- **You could add 150 ml (¼ pint) dry white wine instead of the same quantity of stock.**

- **Don't use highly seasoned stock cubes or they will overpower the delicate saffron flavour. One stock cube dissolved in 1.2 litres (2 pints) boiling water will give plenty of flavour.**

- **Don't keep risotto waiting longer than is absolutely necessary or the rice will go very sticky.**

rice risotto with cod

Squid in puttanesca sauce

The squid takes on the full flavour of the puttanesca, a rich Italian tomato, caper and olive sauce, and almost melts in the mouth. Serve tossed with cooked linguine or another pasta of your choice and a glass of robust red wine.

Serves 4

Preparation time: 25 minutes
Cooking time: 3½–4½ hours
Cooking temperature: low
Slow cooker size: standard

500 g (1 lb) squid tubes and tentacles
1 tablespoon olive oil
1 onion, chopped
2 garlic cloves, finely chopped
400 g (13 oz) can chopped tomatoes
150 ml (¼ pint) fish stock
4 teaspoons capers, drained
50 g (2 oz) pitted black olives
2–3 sprigs of thyme, plus extra to garnish (optional)
1 teaspoon fennel seeds, roughly crushed
1 teaspoon caster sugar
salt and pepper
linguine, to serve

1 Preheat the slow cooker if necessary – see manufacturer's instructions. Take the tentacles out of the squid tubes and rinse inside the tubes with cold water. Put them in a sieve and rinse the outside of the tubes and the tentacles. Drain well, put the tentacles in a small bowl, cover and return to the refrigerator. Thickly slice the squid tubes.

2 Heat the oil in a large frying pan, add the onion and fry, stirring, for 5 minutes or until golden. Add the garlic and cook for 2 minutes. Stir in the tomatoes, stock, capers, olives, thyme, fennel seeds, sugar and salt and pepper and bring to the boil.

3 Transfer the sauce to the slow cooker pot, add the sliced squid and press the pieces below the surface of the sauce. Cover and cook on low for 3–4 hours.

4 Stir the squid mixture and add the squid tentacles, pressing them below the surface of the sauce. Cook on low for 30 minutes. Serve tossed with cooked linguine, and thyme sprigs, if using.

Accompaniments

Spiced red cabbage

Gently braised red cabbage, flavoured with chillies, balsamic vinegar, honey and raisins, is delicious with grilled sausages, mackerel or a roast joint. Replace the honey and fennel seeds with soft light brown sugar and caraway seeds if preferred.

Serves 6

Preparation time: 15 minutes
Cooking time: 2½–3½ hours
Cooking temperature: high
Slow cooker size: standard

1 tablespoon olive oil
1 large onion, chopped
450 ml (¾ pint) hot vegetable or chicken stock
3 tablespoons balsamic vinegar
2 tablespoons thick set honey
1 tablespoon tomato purée
1 teaspoon fennel seeds, roughly crushed
½ teaspoon crushed dried chillies (optional)
625 g (1¼ lb) red cabbage, quartered, cored and thinly sliced
2 dessert apples, cored and diced
50 g (2 oz) raisins
salt and pepper

1 Preheat the slow cooker if necessary – see manufacturer's instructions. Heat the oil in a large frying pan, add the onion and fry, stirring, for 5 minutes until lightly browned. Stir in the stock, vinegar, honey, tomato purée, fennel seeds and crushed dried chillies, if using, then pour into the slow cooker pot.

2 Add the shredded cabbage, apples and raisins. Season well with salt and pepper, mix together, then cover with the lid and cook on high for 2½–3½ hours until the cabbage is tender.

Braised baby carrots
with herb butter

Baby carrots are slowly cooked with stock then finished with a rich green, herb butter made with tarragon and chives – an easy side dish that complements roasted or grilled meats perfectly.

Serves 4–6

Preparation time: 15 minutes
Cooking time: 2–2½ hours
Cooking temperature: high
Slow cooker size: standard

500 g (1 lb) baby carrots, scrubbed and halved
    lengthways if large
250 ml (8 fl oz) hot chicken or vegetable stock
1 teaspoon thick set honey
1 tablespoon tarragon, chopped (optional)
1 tablespoon chives, chopped (optional)
salt and pepper

Herb butter

40 g (1½ oz) butter
1 tablespoon chopped tarragon
2 tablespoons chopped chives
salt and pepper

1 Preheat the slow cooker if necessary – see manufacturer's instructions. Put the carrots in the slow cooker pot with the hot stock, honey, herbs and salt and pepper. Cover with the lid and cook on high for 2–2½ hours until tender.

2 Meanwhile, beat the butter with the herbs and a little salt and pepper. Chill until required. Drain and transfer the carrots to a serving dish, dot the herb butter over the top and serve.

Tips

• **If using carrots still with their green tops on then trim to about 1.5 cm (¾ inch) and weigh after preparation.**

• **Add a little lemon rind and juice to the butter instead of the chives if liked.**

Cheesy vegetable galette

You can transform everyday potatoes and root vegetables by flavouring them with garlic and bathing them in a rich cheesy sauce, ready to serve with grilled chops or fish.

Serves 4–5

Preparation time: 25 minutes
Cooking time: 3–4 hours
Cooking temperature: low
Slow cooker size: standard

50 g (2 oz) butter, plus extra for greasing
50 g (2 oz) plain flour
600 ml (1 pint) full-fat milk
2–3 garlic cloves, finely chopped
100 g (3½ oz) strong Cheddar cheese, grated
625 g (1¼ lb) small baking potatoes,
   peeled and thinly sliced
1 carrot, peeled and thinly sliced
1 parsnip, peeled and thinly sliced
½ large onion, finely chopped
salt and pepper
chopped parsley, to garnish (optional)

1 Preheat the slow cooker if necessary – see manufacturer's instructions. Melt the butter in a saucepan, stir in the flour and cook for 1 minute. Gradually stir in the milk and bring to the boil, stirring continuously until thickened and smooth. Stir in the garlic, three-quarters of the cheese and a little salt and pepper.

2 Brush the inside of the slow cooker pot with a little butter then layer half the root vegetables, potatoes and onion in the pot. Cover with half the cheese sauce then continue layering the vegetables. Pour the remaining hot cheese sauce over the top and sprinkle with the remaining cheese.

3 Cover the cooker with the lid and cook on low for 3–4 hours until the vegetables are tender. Sprinkle with a little chopped parsley, if using, and serve.

Tip
- **While most dishes made in a slow cooker are fine if left to cook longer than the time stated, those made with milk are the exception and must be served within the time specified in the recipe.**

Saffron-baked

Give plain boiled potatoes a lift by cooking them slowly with saffron, garlic and North African spices. Serve with barbecued or grilled meats or with fish steaks.

Serves 6

Preparation time: 15 minutes
Cooking time: 4–5 hours
Cooking temperature: low
Slow cooker size: standard

2 tablespoons olive oil
1 large onion, thinly sliced
1 teaspoon cumin seeds, roughly crushed
1 teaspoon coriander seeds, roughly crushed
large pinch of saffron threads
½ teaspoon turmeric
2 garlic cloves, chopped
450 ml (¾ pint) chicken or vegetable stock
50 g (2 oz) sultanas
½ teaspoon salt
1 kg (2 lb) new potatoes, scrubbed and cut into
   pieces no larger than 4 cm (1½ inch) square
pepper
chopped coriander leaves, to garnish (optional)

1 Preheat the slow cooker if necessary – see manufacturer's instructions. Heat the oil in a frying pan, add the onion and fry, stirring, for 5 minutes until lightly browned.

2 Stir the crushed cumin and coriander seeds into the onion with the saffron, turmeric and garlic and cook for 1 minute. Pour in the stock, then add the sultanas, salt and a little pepper. Bring to the boil, stirring.

3 Pour the onion mixture into the slow cooker pot. Add the potato chunks, making sure they are below the level of the liquid. Cover with the lid and cook on low for 4–5 hours until tender. Transfer to a serving dish and sprinkle with chopped coriander, if using.

Tip
• **Try to cut the potatoes to as similar a size as possible so that they cook evenly – the larger they are, the longer they will take to cook. Old baking potatoes may also be used.**

potatoes

Tamarind lentils
& vegetables

Popular in southern India, this red lentil-based dish is flavoured with root ginger, turmeric and tamarind paste, and finished with fresh coriander. Serve it with rice and meaty curries.

Serves 6

Preparation time: 20 minutes
Cooking time: 7–8 hours
Cooking temperature: low
Slow cooker size: standard

1 tablespoon sunflower oil
1 large onion, chopped
3.5 cm (1½ inch) piece of fresh root ginger, peeled and finely chopped
2–3 garlic cloves, chopped
1 teaspoon turmeric
½ teaspoon crushed dried chillies
2 teaspoons soft light brown sugar
2 teaspoons tamarind paste
900 ml (1½ pints) vegetable stock
175 g (6 oz) red lentils
1 potato, about 250 g (8 oz), diced
2 carrots, diced
small bunch of coriander
salt and pepper

1 Preheat the slow cooker if necessary – see manufacturer's instructions. Heat the oil in a frying pan, add the onion and fry, stirring, for 5 minutes until lightly browned.

2 Stir in the ginger, garlic, turmeric and crushed dried chillies, then add the sugar, tamarind paste and stock. Season with salt and pepper and bring to the boil, stirring.

3 Pour the mixture into the slow cooker pot. Stir in the red lentils and diced vegetables. Cover with the lid and cook on low for 7–8 hours until the lentils are tender. Finely chop about 4 tablespoons of the coriander, stir into the lentils then garnish with the remaining leaves.

Tips

• **Derived from a fruit known as the Indian date, tamarind paste is sold in jars and found in the dry spices section of good supermarkets.**

• **Top the lentils with halved dried chillies and a few curry leaves warmed in a little extra oil or with a little finely chopped fresh red chilli, if liked.**

Coconut & lime rice

Cooking several different dishes at once is much easier if you can leave the rice to cook unattended in the slow cooker. Adding the lime rind and juice at the end of cooking accounts for the intensity of the flavour. Thai rice is a little stickier than basmati rice.

Serves 4

Preparation time: 5 minutes
Cooking time: 1¼–1½ hours
Cooking temperature: high
Slow cooker size: standard

250 g (8 oz) Thai fragrant rice
25 g (1 oz) wild rice
40 g (1½ oz) creamed coconut
600 ml (1 pint) boiling water
grated rind and juice of 2 limes
salt

1 Preheat the slow cooker if necessary – see manufacturer's instructions. Put the Thai and wild rice in a sieve and rinse well under cold running water. Find a large heatproof bowl that will fit comfortably in your slow cooker pot, add the creamed coconut and mix to a paste with a little of the boiling water. Stir in the rest of the water, rinsed rice and salt.

2 Cover the bowl with foil then stand it in the slow cooker pot on top of an upturned saucer. Pour boiling water to come halfway up the sides of the bowl then cover the cooker with its lid. Cook on high for 1¼–1½ hours or until the rice is tender.

3 Fluff up the rice with a fork, draining off any excess liquid. Stir in the lime rind and juice and a little extra boiling water if needed, then serve.

Tip

- If liked, the bowl in which the rice is cooked can be used as a mould. Once the lime rind and juice have been added, press the rice down into the bowl, leave for 5 minutes then run a knife around the inside edge of the bowl to loosen the rice and turn it out on to a plate.

Desserts

White chocolate

bread & butter pudding

This rich creamy custard, buttery bread and just-melted white chocolate is served with a naturally sweet blueberry sauce.

Serves 4–5

Preparation time: 35 minutes
Cooking time: 4–4 1/2 hours
Cooking temperature: low
Slow cooker size: standard

half a French stick, thinly sliced
50 g (2 oz) butter, at room temperature
100 g (3 1/2 oz) white chocolate, chopped
4 egg yolks
50 g (2 oz) caster sugar, plus 3 tablespoons extra for
  caramelizing
150 ml (1/4 pint) double cream
300 ml (1/2 pint) milk
1 teaspoon vanilla essence

Blueberry coulis
125 g (4 oz) blueberries
1 tablespoon caster sugar
4 tablespoons water

To decorate (optional)
few extra blueberries
little white chocolate, diced

1 Preheat the slow cooker if necessary – see manufacturer's instructions. Spread the slices of French bread with the butter. Layer the bread in a 1.2 litre (2 pint) heatproof soufflé dish that will fit comfortably in your slow cooker pot (allowing for a gap of at least 1.5 cm/3/4 inch all the way around), sprinkling the chopped white chocolate between the layers of bread.

2 Beat the egg yolks and sugar together in a bowl with a fork. Pour the cream and milk into a saucepan and bring just to the boil. Gradually stir into the egg mixture, then stir in the vanilla essence.

3 Pour the cream mixture over the layered bread slices and leave to stand for 10 minutes.

4 Cover the top of the soufflé dish with foil then lower into the slow cooker pot, using foil straps or a string pudding bowl lifter (see page 15). Pour hot water around the dish to come halfway up the sides then cover the cooker with the lid and cook on low for 4–4 1/2 hours until the custard has set.

5 Meanwhile, make the blueberry coulis: purée the blueberries with the sugar and water until smooth. Pour into a jug and set aside.

6 Carefully lift the dish out of the slow cooker. Remove the foil and sprinkle the remaining caster sugar over the top of the pudding. Caramelize the sugar under a hot grill or using a cook's blowtorch. To serve, spoon the bread and butter pudding into individual bowls and sprinkle with extra blueberries and white chocolate, if using. Stir the blueberry coulis and pour it around the pudding.

Figgy pudding with cinnamon custard

Serves 6

Preparation time: 30 minutes
Cooking time: 3–3¼ hours
Cooking temperature: high
Slow cooker size: standard

6 tablespoons golden syrup
150 g (5 oz) self-raising flour
½ teaspoon bicarbonate of soda
1 teaspoon ground cinnamon
100 g (3½ oz) shredded suet
50 g (2 oz) fresh breadcrumbs
175 g (6 oz) ready-to-eat dried figs, chopped
50 g (2 oz) ready-to-eat dried apricots, chopped
grated rind and juice of 1 orange
2 eggs, beaten

Cinnamon custard

425 g (14 oz) carton ready-made custard
¼ teaspoon ground cinnamon
2–3 tablespoons sherry

1 Preheat the slow cooker if necessary – see manufacturer's instructions. Lightly butter a 1.2 litre (2 pint) pudding basin that will fit comfortably in your slow cooker pot and line the bottom with a circle of nonstick baking or greaseproof paper. Spoon in 2 tablespoons of the golden syrup.

2 Put the flour, bicarbonate of soda, cinnamon, suet and breadcrumbs in a mixing bowl and mix together. Add the dried fruit, orange rind and juice, eggs and remaining golden syrup and mix together.

3 Spoon the pudding ingredients into the bottom of the prepared basin. Cover with buttered and pleated foil, tie with string and make a string handle (see page 15). Stand the pudding on an upturned saucer in the slow cooker pot then pour boiling water around the basin to come halfway up its sides. Add the cooker lid and cook on high for 3–3¼ hours. Lift the pudding out of the slow cooker and check that it is cooked. It should be well risen and browned, and the top should spring back when pressed with a fingertip.

4 To serve, heat the custard ingredients together in a saucepan, stirring until smooth. Remove the string and foil from the pudding, run a knife around the inside edge of the basin to loosen the pudding then turn it out on to a plate. Remove the lining paper and serve with the hot custard.

Jewelled rice pudding

This quickly made, nursery-style dessert is strictly only suitable for those who are not on a diet! For an extra special touch soak the dried fruits in a little sherry or orange liqueur for 2–3 hours or overnight before using.

Serves 6

Preparation time: 10 minutes
Cooking time: 4–4½ hours
Cooking temperature: low
Slow cooker size: standard

butter, for greasing
900 ml (1½ pints) full-fat milk
75 g (3 oz) pudding rice
75 g (3 oz) caster sugar
1½ teaspoons vanilla essence
50 g (2 oz) ready-to-eat dried apricots, chopped
50 g (2 oz) dried berries and cherries
  (a mix of dried cranberries, blueberries
  and cherries)
grated nutmeg, for sprinkling
extra thick cream and red berry jam, to serve

1 Preheat the slow cooker if necessary – see manufacturer's instructions. Brush the cooker pot with a little butter. Pour the milk into a saucepan, bring just to the boil then pour into the cooker pot.

2 Add the rice, sugar and vanilla essence then stir in the dried fruits. Sprinkle the top with the nutmeg. Cover with the lid and cook on low for 4–4½ hours until the rice is tender. Don't leave the pudding to cook for any longer as you may find that the milk begins to separate.

3 To serve, spoon the rice pudding into individual bowls and top with spoonfuls of extra thick cream and red berry jam.

Sticky orange sponge

This homely, comforting pudding uses ingredients from the storecupboard and fruit bowl, and could be made in the same way with just lemons or lemon and orange.

Serves 4–6

Preparation time: 35 minutes
Cooking time: 3–3½ hours
Cooking temperature: high
Slow cooker size: standard

2 oranges, unpeeled
250 ml (8 fl oz) water
125 g (4 oz) butter, at room temperature, plus
  extra for greasing
200 g (7 oz) caster sugar
3 eggs, beaten
175 g (6 oz) self-raising flour
¼ teaspoon ground cinnamon
3 tablespoons golden syrup
1 tablespoon cornflour

1 Thinly slice 1 of the oranges. Grate the rind and squeeze the juice from the other. Put the sliced orange in a saucepan with the water, cover and simmer for 20 minutes until the orange is tender.

2 Meanwhile, preheat the slow cooker if necessary – see manufacturer's instructions. Butter the inside of a 1.2 litre (2 pint) heatproof pudding basin. Put the remaining butter and 125 g (4 oz) of the sugar in a mixing bowl and beat until light and fluffy using a wooden spoon or an electric mixer. Gradually beat the eggs and flour alternately into the creamed mixture, then stir in half the orange rind and the cinnamon.

3 Lift the cooked orange slices out of the water, reserving the water, then arrange enough slices to cover the bottom and sides of the pudding basin. Spoon in the golden syrup. Add the creamed mixture and smooth the surface flat.

4 Cover with buttered and pleated foil. Tie tightly in place with string, adding a string handle (see page 15). Stand the basin on an upturned saucer in the slow cooker pot then pour boiling water into the pot to come halfway up the sides of the basin. Cover with the lid and cook on high for 3–3½ hours.

5 Meanwhile, make the orange sauce: measure the reserved orange water and juice and make up to 250 ml (8 fl oz) with extra water. Finely chop any remaining cooked orange slices and stir into the juice with the remaining orange rind and sugar. Mix the cornflour to a smooth paste with a little cold water in a saucepan. Add the juice mixure. Bring the sauce to the boil, stirring until thickened and smooth. Strain, if liked.

6 Remove the string and foil from the basin – the pudding should be well risen and the top should spring back when pressed with a fingertip. Run a knife around the inside edge of the basin to loosen the pudding then turn it out on to a plate. Cut into wedges and serve with the warm orange sauce.

pudding with orange sauce

Baked vanilla cheesecake

Serves 6

Preparation time: 45 minutes, plus overnight chilling
Cooking time: 3 hours
Cooking temperature: high
Slow cooker size: large or extra large

Base

50 g (2 oz) butter, at room temperature
50 g (2 oz) caster sugar
50 g (2 oz) self-raising flour
1 egg

Cheesecake

300 g (10 oz) full-fat cream cheese
200 ml (7 fl oz) full-fat crème fraîche
50 g (2 oz) caster sugar
3 eggs, beaten
1 teaspoon vanilla essence
icing sugar, to decorate
mixed berry fruits, to serve

1 Preheat the slow cooker if necessary – see manufacturer's instructions. Line the base and sides of an 18 cm (7 inch) diameter, deep round cake tin with nonstick baking paper – do not use a loose-bottomed tin. Put all the ingredients for the base in a mixing bowl or food processor and beat together until smooth. Spoon into the prepared cake tin, smooth with a knife then cover the top of the tin loosely with foil.

2 Stand the cake tin on an upturned individual tart tin, saucer or biscuit cutter in the slow cooker pot. Pour boiling water into the pot to come halfway up the sides of the cake tin then add the lid and cook on high for 1 hour.

3 Meanwhile, make the cheesecake: put the cream cheese, crème fraîche and sugar in a bowl. Gradually mix in the eggs until smooth then stir in the vanilla essence.

4 Carefully lift the cake tin out of the slow cooker pot using oven gloves. Carefully remove the foil – the sponge layer should be dry and can be pressed with a fingertip. Pour the cheesecake mixture into the tin on top of the cooked sponge, cover again loosely with foil and return to the slow cooker pot. Replace the lid and cook on high for 2 hours until the cheesecake can be touched lightly with fingertips.

5 Switch off the slow cooker, remove the foil and leave the cheesecake to cool, still in the hot water. Don't be alarmed to see that the cheesecake will sink on cooling – this is normal. When the water is barely warm, lift out the tin out, transfer to the refrigerator and chill overnight to achieve the characteristic baked cheesecake texture.

6 Carefully remove the cheesecake from the cake tin, peel off the lining paper and place on a serving plate. Dust liberally with icing sugar and serve with mixed berry fruits.

Tip
- **Before you begin, check that the cake tin you intend to use fits comfortably into your slow cooker pot. Do not use a loose-bottomed cake tin or the water will seep into the cheesecake during cooking – if the seal on the cake tin is not watertight, stand it in a large dish or sandwich tin.**

Classic crème brûlée

Crack through the thin, brittle caramelized sugar topping to reveal a rich and velvety vanilla custard. Although this dessert is served in many smart restaurants, it is surprisingly easy to make at home, especially in a slow cooker.

Serves 4

Preparation time: 30 minutes, plus chilling
Cooking time: 3–3½ hours
Cooking temperature: low
Slow cooker size: standard

½ vanilla pod
400 ml (14 fl oz) double cream
5 egg yolks
40 g (1½ oz) caster sugar
2 tablespoons icing sugar, for caramelizing
selection of berry fruits, to serve

1 Preheat the slow cooker if necessary – see manufacturer's instructions. Slit the vanilla pod along its length then place in a saucepan with the cream. Bring the cream just to the boil then remove from the heat and leave for 20 minutes to allow the flavours to infuse.

2 Mix the egg yolks and sugar together in a bowl using a fork. Lift the vanilla pod out of the cream, scrape the black seeds away from inside the pod and add them to the cream. Reheat the cream until almost boiling then gradually stir into the egg mixture. Strain into a jug.

3 Pour the mixture into 4 x 150 ml (¼ pint) heatproof ramekin dishes then stand the dishes in the slow cooker pot – there is no need to cover them with foil. Pour hot water around the dishes to come halfway up their sides, taking care not to splash any water into the cream. Cover the cooker with the lid and cook on low for 3–3½ hours until the desserts are set, with a slight quiver to their centres.

4 Carefully lift the cooker pot out of the base unit using oven gloves. Leave to cool at room temperature then lift out the ramekin dishes and transfer to the refrigerator for at least 4 hours until well chilled.

5 Just before serving, sprinkle the top of the desserts with icing sugar (there is no need to sift it) then caramelize the sugar using a cook's blowtorch. If you don't have a blowtorch then arrange the ramekin dishes in a small roasting tin, half-fill it with cold water and add ice cubes. Place the tin under a hot grill, getting the tops of the ramekin dishes as close to the heat as you can, to caramelize the sugar topping.

6 To serve, stand the ramekin dishes on small plates and decorate with berry fruits. Serve within 20 minutes.

Poached peaches

Fresh peaches are delicious eaten raw but can go mouldy quickly. Capture them at their best by cooking them in this Italian-inspired sugar syrup, flavoured with marsala and vanilla, for an effortless but elegant dessert.

Serves 4–6

Preparation time: 15 minutes
Cooking time: 1¼–1¾ hours
Cooking temperature: low and high
Slow cooker size: standard

150 ml (¼ pint) marsala or sweet sherry
150 ml (¼ pint) water
75 g (3 oz) caster sugar
6 firm ripe peaches or nectarines,
   halved and stones removed
1 vanilla pod, slit lengthways
2 teaspoons cornflour
125 g (4 oz) fresh raspberries
crème fraîche, to serve

1 Preheat the slow cooker if necessary – see manufacturer's instructions. Put the marsala or sherry, the water and sugar in a saucepan and bring to the boil.

2 Place the peach or nectarine halves and vanilla pod in the slow cooker pot and pour in the hot syrup. Cover with the lid and cook on low for 1–1½ hours until hot and tender.

3 Lift the fruit out of the slow cooker pot and place in a serving dish. Remove the vanilla pod then scrape the black seeds from the pod with a small sharp knife and stir the seeds back into the cooking syrup. Mix the cornflour to a smooth paste with a little cold water, then stir into the cooking syrup and cook on high for 15 minutes, stirring occasionally.

4 Pour the thickened syrup over the peaches, sprinkle with the raspberries and serve warm or chilled with spoonfuls of crème fraîche.

Tips

• **This dish is equally delicious served with vanilla ice cream or mascarpone cheese, or with whipped cream flavoured with crushed amaretti or ratafia biscuits.**

• **To make in a larger slow cooker, increase the ingredient quantities by half as much again.**

with marsala & vanilla

Serves 6–8

Preparation time: 40 minutes
Cooking time: 2–2½ hours
Cooking temperature: high
Slow cooker size: large or extra large

50 g (2 oz) cocoa powder
6 tablespoons boiling water
175 g (6 oz) self-raising flour
1½ teaspoons baking powder
150 g (5 oz) caster sugar
150 ml (¼ pint) sunflower oil
3 eggs

To finish

4 tablespoons chocolate and hazelnut spread
450 ml (¾ pint) double cream
white chocolate curls (see Tip)
little sifted cocoa

1 Preheat the slow cooker if necessary – see manufacturer's instructions. Line the bottom and sides of an 18 cm (7 inch) diameter, deep round cake tin with nonstick baking paper – do not use a loose-bottomed tin. Put the cocoa in a small bowl and gradually mix to a smooth paste with the boiling water. Leave to cool.

Tips

- **Before you begin make sure that the cake tin will fit in the slow cooker pot and that it is wateright.**
- **To make chocolate curls, run a swivel-bladed vegetable peeler along the edge of a block of chocolate that has been stored at room temperature.**

2 Put the flour, baking powder and sugar in a mixing bowl and mix well. Beat together the oil and eggs then add to the dry ingredients. Spoon in the cocoa paste and mix together until smooth.

3 Pour the cake mixture into the prepared cake tin, smooth with a knife then cover the top of the tin loosely with foil. Stand the cake tin on an upturned saucer or individual tart tin in the slow cooker pot. Pour boiling water into the pot to come halfway up the sides of the cake tin. Cover with the lid and cook on high for 2–2½ hours, or until the cake is well risen, the top is dry and a skewer inserted into the centre comes out clean.

4 Carefully lift the cake tin out of the slow cooker pot using oven gloves. Remove the cake from the tin and turn it out on to a wire rack. Peel off the lining paper and leave to cool.

5 Just before serving, split the cake into three layers. Place the bottom layer on a serving plate and spread with half the chocolate and hazelnut spread. Whip the cream until it just holds its shape, spoon a little of the cream over the chocolate spread and smooth with a knife. Top with the another cake layer, spread with more chocolate spread and cream. Add the last layer of cake and spread the remaining cream over the top and sides of the cake. Sprinkle with white chocolate curls and dust with a little cocoa.

chocolate cake

Dark chocolate pots

with coffee cream liqueur

This dessert is simple to create, yet wonderfully decadent. Do check that the small pots or mugs fit in your slow cooker before you begin. Use milk chocolate instead of dark if preferred.

Serves 4

Preparation time: 25 minutes, plus chilling
Cooking time: 3–3½ hours
Cooking temperature: low
Slow cooker size: standard

450 ml (¾ pint) full-fat milk
150 ml (¼ pint) double cream
200 g (7 oz) dark chocolate, broken into pieces
2 whole eggs
3 egg yolks
50 g (2 oz) caster sugar
¼ teaspoon ground cinnamon

Topping

150 ml (¼ pint) double cream
75 ml (3 fl oz) coffee cream liqueur
chocolate curls, to decorate

1 Preheat the slow cooker if necessary – see manufacturer's instructions. Pour the milk and cream into a saucepan and bring just to the boil. Remove from the heat, add the chocolate pieces and set aside for 5 minutes, stirring occasionally until the chocolate has melted.

2 Put the whole eggs, egg yolks, sugar and cinnamon in a mixing bowl and whisk until smooth. Gradually whisk in the warm chocolate milk, then strain the mixture into 4 x 250 ml (8 fl oz) heatproof pots or mugs.

3 Cover the tops of the pots or mugs with foil then stand them in the slow cooker pot. Pour hot water into the slow cooker pot to come halfway up the sides of the pots or mugs. Cover the cooker with the lid and cook on low for 3–3½ hours until set.

4 Carefully lift the dishes out of the slow cooker pot using oven gloves. Leave to cool at room temperature then transfer to the refrigerator for at least 4 hours until well chilled.

5 Just before serving, whip the cream until soft swirls form. Gradually whisk in the liqueur then spoon the flavoured cream over the top of the desserts. Sprinkle with chocolate curls and serve.

This continental-style cake, which doubles as a dessert if served with cream, is made with ground almonds and polenta instead of wheat flour so is ideal for anyone on a wheat-free diet.

Serves 6

Preparation time: 30 minutes
Cooking time: 3–3½ hours
Cooking temperature: high
Slow cooker size: large or extra large

150 g (5 oz) butter, at room temperature,
   plus extra for greasing
200 g (7 oz) sweet red plums, thickly sliced
150 g (5 oz) caster sugar
2 eggs, beaten
100 g (3½ oz) ground almonds
50 g (2 oz) fine polenta (cornmeal)
½ teaspoon baking powder
grated rind and juice of ½ orange
whipped cream, to serve (optional)

To decorate

2 tablespoons toasted flaked almonds
sifted icing sugar

1 Preheat the slow cooker if necessary – see manufacturer's instructions. Butter a 1.2 litre (2 pint) oval or round heatproof dish that will fit comfortably in your slow cooker pot and line the bottom with a piece of nonstick baking or greaseproof paper. Arrange the plum halves, cut side down, in rings in the base of the dish.

2 Cream the remaining butter and sugar together in a mixing bowl until light and fluffy. Gradually beat the eggs and ground almonds alternately into the butter mixture. Stir in the polenta, baking powder, orange rind and juice and beat until smooth.

3 Spoon the cake mixture over the plums and smooth with a knife. Cover the dish with buttered foil then stand it on an upturned saucer or 2 individual flan rings in the slow cooker pot. Pour boiling water into the pot to come halfway up the sides of the dish. Add the cooker lid then cook on high for 3–3½ hours, or until the top of the cake is dry and springs back when pressed with a fingertip.

4 Carefully remove the dish from the slow cooker using oven gloves. Take off the foil and leave to cool slightly then run a knife around the inside edge of the dish to loosen the cake and turn it out on to a serving plate. Remove the lining paper, sprinkle the top with toasted flaked almonds and dust with a little sifted icing sugar to decorate. Cut into wedges and serve warm or cold with spoonfuls of whipped cream.

Sticky toffee

Serves 4–5

Preparation time: 30 minutes
Cooking time: 3–3½ hours
Cooking temperature: high
Slow cooker size: standard

50 g (2 oz) butter, diced, plus extra for greasing
150 g (5 oz) self-raising flour
100 g (3½ oz) dark muscovado sugar
2 eggs
2 tablespoons milk
1 dessert apple, cored and finely chopped
vanilla ice cream, crème fraîche or pouring cream,
  to serve

Sauce
125 g (4 oz) dark muscovado sugar
25 g (1 oz) butter, diced
300 ml (½ pint) boiling water

1 Preheat the slow cooker if necessary – see manufacturer's instructions. Butter the inside of a soufflé dish that is 14 cm (5½ inches) across and 9 cm (3½ inches) high. Put the flour in a bowl, add the butter and rub in with the fingertips until the mixture resembles fine breadcrumbs. Stir in the sugar, then mix in the eggs and milk until smooth. Stir in the apple.

2 Spoon the mixture into the soufflé dish and spread it level. Sprinkle the sugar for the sauce over the top and dot with the 25 g (1 oz) butter. Pour the measured boiling water over the top, then loosely cover with foil.

3 Carefully lower the dish into the slow cooker pot using a string handle or foil straps (see page 15). Pour boiling water into the pot so that it comes halfway up the sides of the soufflé dish. Cover and cook on high for 3–3½ hours or until the sponge is well risen and the sauce is bubbling around the edges.

4 Lift the dish out of the slow cooker. Remove the foil and loosen the sides of the sponge. Cover with a dish that is large enough to catch the sauce, invert and remove the soufflé dish. Serve with spoonfuls of vanilla ice cream, crème fraîche or pouring cream.

Tip
• **Check that the soufflé dish will fit in your slow cooker pot before you begin.**

Rum and raisin spotted dick

Serves 8

Preparation time: 20 minutes, plus soaking
Cooking time: 3–4 hours
Cooking temperature: high
Slow cooker size: standard

200 g (7 oz) raisins
5 tablespoons dark rum
butter, for greasing
200 g (7 oz) self-raising flour
50 g (2 oz) fresh white breadcrumbs
100 g (3½ oz) light vegetable suet
100 g (3½ oz) caster sugar
finely grated rind and juice of 1 orange
1 egg
150 ml (¼ pint) milk

To serve
golden syrup
custard

1 Put the raisins in a bowl, add the rum and leave to soak overnight.

2 Preheat the slow cooker if necessary – see manufacturer's instructions. Butter a 1.25 litre (2¼ pint) pudding basin and line the base with a circle of greaseproof paper. Put the flour, breadcrumbs, suet, sugar and orange rind in a mixing bowl. Add the raisins and any remaining rum, the orange juice and egg, then gradually mix in enough milk to make a soft, dropping consistency.

3 Spoon the mixture into the basin, level the surface and cover with a piece of pleated greaseproof paper and foil. Tie the foil in place with string and lower the basin into the base of the slow cooker pot using string handles (see page 15). Pour boiling water into the slow cooker pot so that it comes halfway up the side of the basin, cover and cook on high for 3–4 hours or until the pudding is well risen and cooked through.

4 Loosen the sides of the pudding, turn it out on to a plate and peel away the lining paper. Serve with golden syrup and custard.

Tips

• **If you're short of time, warm the rum and raisins in a saucepan or in the microwave and leave to soak for 2 hours.**

• **When there's not enough bread to make into breadcrumbs, use 275 g (9 oz) self-raising flour, although the texture of the pudding will be a little heavier.**

Butterscotch bananas

This children's favourite is incredibly quick and easy to make, and it's likely that you will already have all the necessary ingredients in your storecupboard.

Serves 4
Preparation time: 15 minutes
Cooking time: 1–1½ hours
Cooking temperature: low
Slow cooker size: standard

4 bananas
juice of 1 lemon
50 g (2 oz) butter
75 g (3 oz) soft light brown muscovado sugar
2 tablespoons golden syrup
vanilla ice cream, to serve

1 Preheat the slow cooker if necessary – see manufacturer's instructions. Thickly slice the bananas, put them in a bowl and toss with the lemon juice.

2 Put the butter, sugar and syrup in a small saucepan and heat until the butter has melted and the sugar has dissolved.

3 Transfer the bananas to the slow cooker pot, pour the hot butter mixture over them, cover and cook on low for 1–1½ hours.

4 Spoon the bananas into glass bowls and serve with scoops of vanilla ice cream.

Black cherry &

These irresistible little puddings are made easily with a quick-mix sponge and a can of cherries from your storecupboard.

Serves 4

Preparation time: 25 minutes
Cooking time: 1½–2 hours
Cooking temperature: high
Slow cooker size: standard

50 g (2 oz) butter, plus extra for greasing
50 g (2 oz) caster sugar
50 g (2 oz) self-raising flour
1 egg
1 tablespoon cocoa powder
¼ teaspoon baking powder
¼ teaspoon ground cinnamon
425 g (14 oz) can pitted black cherries, drained

Chocolate sauce
100 g (3½ oz) white chocolate, broken into pieces
150 ml (¼ pint) double cream

1 Preheat the slow cooker if necessary – see manufacturer's instructions. Butter the inside of 4 metal pudding moulds, each with a capacity of 200 ml (7 fl oz), and line the base of each with a circle of greaseproof paper.

2 Put the remaining butter, sugar, flour, egg, cocoa, baking powder and cinnamon in a bowl and beat them together with a wooden spoon until smooth.

3 Arrange 7 cherries in the base of each pudding mould. Roughly chop the remainder and stir them into the pudding mix. Divide the mixture among the pudding moulds and level the tops. Loosely cover the tops of the moulds with foil and put them in the slow cooker pot. Pour boiling water into the pot so that it comes halfway up the sides of the moulds, cover and cook on high for 1½–2 hours or until the puddings are well risen and the tops spring back when pressed with a fingertip. Lift the puddings out of the slow cooker pot.

4 Make the sauce. Put the chocolate and cream in a small saucepan and heat gently, stirring occasionally, until melted. Loosen the edges of the puddings, turn them out into shallow bowls, peel away the lining paper and pour the sauce around them before serving.

Tip
• **If you don't have metal moulds, you could use small teacups or coffee cups to cook the puddings but make sure that they fit into the slow cooker pot before you begin.**

Orange risotto with

This Italian dairy-free version of rice pudding is flavoured with an orange syrup and topped with flaked almonds, which have been caramelized with a little icing sugar.

Serves 6

Preparation time: 25 minutes
Cooking time: 2½–3 hours
Cooking temperature: low
Slow cooker size: standard

5 oranges
75 g (3 oz) caster sugar
1–2 bay leaves, depending on size
1 litre (1¾ pints) water
200 g (7 oz) risotto rice
pouring cream, to serve (optional)

Caramelized almonds
15 g (½ oz) butter
40 g (1½ oz) flaked almonds
2 tablespoons icing sugar

1 Preheat the slow cooker if necessary – see manufacturer's instructions. Grate the rind from 1 orange and squeeze the juice from this and another orange. Cut the peel and pith away from the 3 remaining oranges and cut the flesh into segments. Put the segments in a small bowl, cover and set aside until ready to serve.

2 Put the orange rind and juice in a saucepan with the sugar, bay leaves and water. Bring slowly to the boil, stirring, until the sugar has completely dissolved. Boil for 1 minute.

3 Put the rice in the slow cooker pot, pour over the hot syrup and mix together. Cover and cook on low for 2½–3 hours or until the rice is tender and has absorbed most of the syrup.

4 Meanwhile, make the caramelized almonds. Melt the butter in a frying pan, add the almonds and fry, stirring, for 2–3 minutes or until golden. Mix in the sugar and cook for 1 minute.

5 Spoon the risotto into small bowls and top with the orange segments and warm nuts. Serve with a drizzle of pouring cream, if liked.

caramelized almonds

Nectarine compote

with orange mascarpone

Full of summer flavours, these lightly poached fruits are served with soft creamy mascarpone cheese flecked with crumbled almondy amaretti biscuits. Although this compote is served warm here, it tastes just as good chilled.

Serves 4

Preparation time: 20 minutes
Cooking time: 1–1¼ hours
Cooking temperature: high
Slow cooker size: standard

4 nectarines
250 g (8 oz) strawberries
50 g (2 oz) caster sugar, plus 2 tablespoons
finely grated rind and juice of 2 oranges
125 ml (4 fl oz) cold water
150 g (5 oz) mascarpone cheese
40 g (1½ oz) amaretti biscuits

1 Preheat the slow cooker if necessary – see manufacturer's instructions. Halve the nectarines, remove the stones and cut the flesh into chunks. Quarter or halve the strawberries depending on their size.

2 Put the fruit in the slow cooker pot with 50 g (2 oz) sugar, the rind of 1 orange, the juice of 1½ oranges and the measured water. Cover and cook on high for 1–1¼ hours or until the fruit is tender.

3 Just before the compote is ready, mix the mascarpone cheese with the remaining sugar, orange rind and juice. Reserve some of the amaretti biscuits for decoration. Crumble the rest with your fingertips into the bowl with the mascarpone and stir until mixed. Spoon the fruit into tumblers, top with spoonfuls of the mascarpone mixture and decorate with a sprinkling of amaretti biscuits.

Tip
• **Use ratafia or macaroon biscuits instead of the amaretti biscuits if you prefer.**

Lemon sponge pudding

Serves 6

Preparation time: 30 minutes
Cooking time: 3–3½ hours
Cooking temperature: high
Slow cooker size: standard

125 g (4 oz) butter, plus extra for greasing
4 tablespoons golden syrup
100 g (3½ oz) caster sugar
grated rind of 2 lemons
2 eggs, beaten
200 g (7 oz) self-raising flour
2 tablespoons milk
2 tablespoons lemon juice
3 passion fruit

1 Preheat the slow cooker if necessary – see manufacturer's instructions. Butter the inside of a 1.25 litre (2¼ pint) pudding basin and line the base with a circle of greaseproof paper. Spoon the syrup into the basin.

2 Cream together the butter, sugar and lemon rind in a bowl until pale and creamy. Gradually mix in alternate spoonfuls of beaten egg and flour until both have been added and the mixture is smooth. Stir in the milk and then the lemon juice to make a soft, dropping consistency.

3 Spoon the mixture over the syrup in the basin. Level the surface and cover with a piece of pleated greaseproof paper and foil. Tie with string.

4 Lower the basin into the slow cooker pot (see page 15). Pour boiling water into the pot so that it comes halfway up the sides of the basin. Cover and cook on high for 3–3½ hours or until the top springs back when pressed with a fingertip.

5 Carefully lift the basin out of the slow cooker. Remove the foil and greaseproof paper and loosen the sides of the sponge. Cover with a large plate, invert the basin on to it and remove the basin and lining paper. Halve the passion fruit and scoop the seeds over the pudding.

Tip
- **For an alternative sauce, warm 4 tablespoons cranberry sauce or good strawberry jam with the juice of half an orange.**

Double chocolate
& sweet potato cake

Serves 6

Preparation time: 40 minutes
Cooking time: 3½–4 hours
Cooking temperature: high
Slow cooker size: standard

250 g (8 oz) sweet potato, peeled and cut into
  chunks
2 tablespoons milk
125 g (4 oz) butter, plus extra for greasing
125 g (4 oz) soft light muscovado sugar
150 g (5 oz) self-raising flour
2 tablespoons cocoa powder, plus extra to
  decorate (optional)
½ teaspoon bicarbonate of soda
2 eggs, beaten
25 g (1 oz) crystallized ginger, chopped
100 g (3½ oz) dark chocolate, diced
25 g (1 oz) pistachio nuts or hazelnuts, roughly
  chopped
cream, to serve

1 Cook the sweet potato in a saucepan of boiling water for 15 minutes or until tender. Drain and mash with the milk, then leave to cool.

2 Preheat the slow cooker if necessary – see manufacturer's instructions. Butter the inside of a soufflé dish that is 14 cm (5½ inches) across and 9 cm (3½ inches) high, and line the base with greaseproof paper. Cream the butter and sugar together in a bowl until light and fluffy. Mix the flour, cocoa and bicarbonate of soda together. Gradually mix in alternate spoonfuls of egg and flour until both have been added and the mixture is smooth. Stir in the potato, ginger and chocolate.

3 Spoon the mixture into the buttered dish, level the surface and sprinkle over the nuts. Cover the top loosely with buttered foil and lower into the slow cooker pot (see page 15). Pour boiling water into the pot so that it comes halfway up the sides of the dish. Cover and cook on high for 3½–4 hours or until the cake springs back when pressed with a fingertip.

4 Loosen the cake, turn it out on to a plate and peel off the lining paper. Serve warm or cold with cream.

Marbled chocolate & vanilla cheesecake

Serves 6

Preparation time: 40 minutes, plus chilling
Cooking time: 3–4 hours
Cooking temperature: high
Slow cooker size: standard

Base

50 g (2 oz) butter at room temperature, plus
  extra for greasing
50 g (2 oz) caster sugar
50 g (2 oz) self-raising flour
1 egg

Filling

100 g (3½ oz) dark chocolate, broken into pieces
250 g (8 oz) mascarpone cheese
50 g (2 oz) caster sugar
4 tablespoons full-fat crème fraîche
2 whole eggs and 2 extra yolks
1 teaspoon vanilla essence

1 Preheat the slow cooker if necessary – see manufacturer's instructions. Butter a soufflé dish that is 14 cm (5½ inches) across and 9 cm (3½ inches) high. Line the base with greaseproof paper.

2 Make the base. Put all the ingredients in a bowl and beat together until smooth. Spoon into the dish and level the surface. Cover the top loosely with foil and lower the dish into the slow cooker pot (see page 15). Pour boiling water into the pot so that it comes halfway up the sides of the dish, cover and cook on high for 1–1½ hours. Meanwhile, melt the chocolate for the filling in a heatproof bowl set over a small saucepan of simmering water. Mix the mascarpone and sugar in another bowl. Stir in the crème fraîche then gradually beat in the whole eggs, and yolks.

3 Lift the dish out of the slow cooker. Gradually stir 8 tablespoons of the cheesecake mixture into the chocolate. Stir the vanilla extract into the remaining mixture, then pour it into the sponge-lined dish. Drizzle spoonfuls of the chocolate mixture over the top, then run a knife through the mixtures to create a marbled effect. Re-cover the dish and return it to the slow cooker. Cook on high for 2–2½ hours. Lift out and cool, then refrigerate for 3–4 hours.

4 Loosen the edges of the cheesecake, turn it out, peel away the paper then turn the right way up.

Tip
• **The cheesecake will sink slightly as it cools. Don't worry – this is perfectly normal.**

Lemon custard creams

Serve this rich baked custard, made with double cream and tangy lemon rind and juice, with your preferred choice of fresh blueberries, mixed summer fruits or cherries.

Serves 6

Preparation time: 15 minutes, plus chilling
Cooking time: 2–2½ hours
Cooking temperature: low
Slow cooker size: standard

2 whole eggs and 3 extra yolks
100 g (3½ oz) caster sugar
grated rind of 2 lemons
juice of 1 lemon
300 ml (½ pint) double cream
150 g (5 oz) fresh blueberries, to serve

1 Preheat the slow cooker if necessary – see manufacturer's instructions. Put the eggs and yolks, sugar and lemon rind in a bowl and whisk together until just mixed.

2 Pour the cream into a small saucepan, bring just to the boil, then gradually whisk it into the egg mixture. Strain the lemon juice and gradually whisk it into the cream mixture.

3 Pour the mixture into 6 small coffee cups and put them in the slow cooker pot. Pour boiling water into the pot so that it comes halfway up the sides of the cups. Loosely cover the tops of the cups with a piece of foil, cover and cook on low for 2–2½ hours or until the custards are just set.

4 Lift the cups from the slow cooker, leave to cool, then transfer to the refrigerator and chill well.

5 To serve, set the cups on their saucers and decorate the tops of the custard with blueberries.

Tips

- **Check that the cups will fit side by side in the pot before you begin. If you don't have any small cups, use dariole or madeleine tins or small 150 ml (¼ pint) metal moulds instead.**

- **To make these desserts into crème brûlée, sprinkle the top of each chilled dessert with 1 rounded teaspoon of caster sugar. Caramelize the sugar with a kitchen blowtorch and serve within 20 minutes.**

Sticky glazed banana

Serves 6

Preparation time: 30 minutes
Cooking time: 4–5 hours
Cooking temperature: high
Slow cooker size: standard

Pudding base

3 tablespoons golden syrup
3 tablespoons light muscovado sugar
1 tablespoon ginger or orange marmalade
2 bananas
juice ½ lemon

Gingerbread

100 g (3½ oz) butter, plus extra for greasing
100 g (3½ oz) light muscovado sugar
75 g (3 oz) golden syrup
2 tablespoons ginger or orange marmalade
2 eggs
4 tablespoons milk
175 g (6 oz) self-raising wholemeal flour
1 teaspoon bicarbonate of soda
2 teaspoons ground ginger
custard or vanilla ice cream, to serve

1 Preheat the slow cooker if necessary – see manufacturer's instructions. Butter a soufflé dish that is 14 cm (5½ inches) in diameter and 9 cm (3½ inches) high and line the base with a circle of greaseproof paper.

2 Make the pudding base. Spoon the syrup, sugar and marmalade into the dish. Cut the bananas in half lengthways, then cut each piece in half again crossways. Toss in the lemon juice and arrange the pieces, cut side down, in the dish.

3 Make the gingerbread. Put the butter, sugar, syrup and marmalade in a saucepan and heat gently until melted. Beat the eggs and milk together in a small bowl and combine the flour, bicarbonate and ginger in another small bowl.

4 Take the pan off the heat and gradually mix in the egg and milk mixture, then the flour mixture until smooth. Pour over the bananas in the dish. Cover the top loosely with foil. Lower the dish into the slow cooker pot (see page 15). Pour boiling water into the gap between the dish and the pot so that it comes halfway up the sides of the dish, cover and cook on high for 4–5 hours or until the top springs back when pressed with a fingertip.

5 Lift out of the slow cooker, remove the foil, loosen the sides of the pudding then cover with a plate and invert on to the plate. Shake smartly to release, carefully remove the dish and peel away the lining paper. Serve with custard or vanilla ice cream.

gingerbread

Poached orchard
fruits with star anise

This light fresh blend of just-cooked fruits is also delicious served chilled for breakfast, topped with spoonfuls of yogurt.

Serves 6
Preparation time: 20 minutes
Cooking time: 2½–3 hours
Cooking temperature: high
Slow cooker size: standard

100 g (3½ oz) caster sugar
300 ml (½ pint) water
3 star anise
grated rind and juice of 1 lemon
300 ml (½ pint) cranberry and raspberry juice
3 pears
2 dessert apples
400 g (13 oz) red plums
Greek yogurt drizzled with honey, to serve

1 Preheat the slow cooker if necessary – see manufacturer's instructions. Put the sugar, measured water, star anise and lemon rind and juice into a saucepan. Heat gently until the sugar has dissolved, then boil for 1 minute. Add the cranberry and raspberry fruit juice and reheat.

2 Quarter, core and peel the pears and apples and cut each apple piece in half again. Halve and stone the plums. Put the fruit in the slow cooker pot and pour over the hot syrup. Cover and cook on high for 2½–3 hours or until the fruits are tender.

3 Serve warm or cold with spoonfuls of Greek yogurt drizzled with honey.

Tip
• **Warn your diners not to eat the star anise.**

Tom

Coconut & lime rice pudding

This new twist on an old favourite pudding is made with reduced-fat coconut milk, sugar and lime rind. Serve topped with mango slices and scoops of crème fraîche.

Serves 4

Preparation time: 15 minutes
Cooking time: 7–8 hours
Cooking temperature: low
Slow cooker size: standard

400 ml (14 fl oz) can coconut milk
450 ml (¾ pint) full-fat milk
butter, for greasing
75 g (3 oz) pudding rice
50 g (2 oz) caster sugar
grated rind of 2 limes

To serve

1 mango, stoned, peeled and diced
juice of 1 lime
crème fraîche

1 Preheat the slow cooker if necessary – see manufacturer's instructions. Pour the coconut milk and full-fat milk into a saucepan and bring just to the boil.

2 Butter the inside of the slow cooker pot and add the rice, sugar and lime rind. Pour the hot milk over the rice and stir to mix. Cover and cook on low for 7–8 hours, stirring once or twice if possible, until the rice is soft and has absorbed most of the milk.

3 Toss the mango pieces in lime juice. Spoon the pudding into bowls and serve topped with crème fraîche and mango.

Tips

- **This version of rice pudding is more like one cooked on the hob, so it is perfect for people who like rice pudding but who hate the skin.**

- **For a change, flavour the pudding with 3 tablespoons of set honey, a little grated nutmeg and 900 ml (1½ pints) full-fat milk instead of the mixture of coconut and dairy milk, sugar and lime.**

Poached apricots

Although adding pepper to a dessert may sound a little strange, it adds a hot spiciness that complements the dryness of the sherry. Any leftover apricots can be puréed and swirled through Greek yogurt for a tasty breakfast.

Serves 4

Preparation time: 5 minutes
Cooking time: 3–4 hours
Cooking temperature: low
Slow cooker size: standard

300 g (10 oz) ready-to-eat dried apricots
150 ml (¼ pint) dry sherry
150 ml (¼ pint) cold water
50 g (2 oz) caster sugar
½ teaspoon black peppercorns, roughly crushed
crème fraîche or vanilla ice cream, to serve

1 Preheat the slow cooker if necessary – see manufacturer's instructions. Put the apricots, sherry and measured water into the slow cooker pot. Sprinkle over the sugar and peppercorns. Cover and cook on low for 3–4 hours or until the apricots are plump and piping hot.

2 Spoon the apricots into glass tumblers and serve hot with spoonfuls of crème fraîche or vanilla ice cream.

Tip
• **You can cook fresh apricots with the same flavourings. Use 500 g (1 lb) fruit and leave whole, or halve and remove the stones if preferred. Cook for 2 hours.**

with cracked pepper

Mini coffee sponge

puddings with coffee liqueur

Serves 4

Preparation time: 30 minutes
Cooking time: 2–2½ hours
Cooking temperature: high
Slow cooker size: standard

100 g (3½ oz) butter, plus extra for greasing
50 g (2 oz) pecan nuts
2 teaspoons instant coffee
3 teaspoons boiling water
100 g (3½ oz) soft light muscovado sugar
2 eggs, beaten
125 g (4 oz) self-raising flour
40 g (1½ oz) dark chocolate

To serve
4 tablespoons double cream
4 tablespoons coffee cream liqueur

1 Preheat the slow cooker if necessary – see manufacturer's instructions. Lightly butter 4 metal moulds, each with a capacity of 200 ml (7 fl oz), and line the bases with circles of greaseproof paper. Arrange 3 pecan nuts in the base of each mould, then break the remaining nuts into pieces with your fingertips. Put the coffee in a cup and stir in the measured boiling water until dissolved.

2 Put the butter and sugar in a bowl and cream them together with a wooden spoon until light and fluffy. Gradually mix in alternate spoonfuls of beaten egg and flour until both have been added.

3 Stir in the broken nuts and the dissolved coffee, then spoon half the mixture into the buttered moulds. Cut the chocolate into 4 pieces and press a piece into each mould. Cover with the remaining coffee mixture and smooth the tops.

4 Cover each pudding with a piece of buttered foil and transfer the puddings to the slow cooker. Pour boiling water into the pot so that it comes halfway up the sides of the moulds, cover and cook on high for 2–2½ hours or until the tops spring back when pressed with a fingertip.

5 Turn out the puddings into shallow bowls, remove the lining paper and spoon the cream and liqueur around the bases.

Tip
- **For a double chocolate pudding, replace 1 tablespoon flour with 1 tablespoon cocoa powder and omit the dissolved coffee.**

Chutneys & conserves

& garlic chutney

Perk up a simple ham or cheese sandwich with this tasty chutney. If you are not a fan of spicy food then simply leave out the chillies, but if you like your food extra hot, use the chilli seeds as well.

Makes 5 x 400 g (13 oz) jars
Preparation time: 30 minutes
Cooking time: 6–8 hours
Cooking temperature: high
Slow cooker size: standard

1 kg (2 lb) tomatoes, skinned and roughly chopped
1 large onion, chopped
2 cooking apples, about 500 g (1 lb), peeled, cored and chopped
2 red peppers, cored, deseeded and diced
75 g (3 oz) sultanas
100 ml (3½ fl oz) distilled malt vinegar
250 g (8 oz) granulated sugar
2–3 large mild red chillies, halved, deseeded and finely chopped
6–8 garlic cloves, finely chopped
1 cinnamon stick, halved
½ teaspoon ground allspice
1 teaspoon salt
pepper

1 Preheat the slow cooker if necessary – see manufacturer's instructions. Put all the ingredients in the slow cooker pot, mix together then cover with the lid and cook on high for 6–8 hours until thick and pulpy.

2 Warm 5 clean jars in the bottom of a low oven. Spoon in the chutney, place a waxed disc on top and leave to cool. Seal each jar with a screw-topped lid then label. Store in a cool place for up to 2 months. Once opened, store in the refrigerator.

Tip
- **Don't worry if your slow cooker pot is very full as the tomatoes will quickly lose their bulk once cooking begins.**

Spiced mango
chutney

This sweet, fruity chutney can be partnered with cheese for a tasty salad or served with poppadums and raita as a starter for a spicy Indian meal.

Makes 3 x 400 g (13 oz) jars

Preparation time: 30 minutes
Cooking time: 2½–2¾ hours
Cooking temperature: high
Slow cooker size: standard

1 large mango
1 small butternut squash, about 750 g (1½ lb), deseeded, peeled and diced
2 large onions, chopped
200 g (7 oz) soft light brown sugar
100 ml (3½ fl oz) white wine vinegar
4 cm (1½ in) piece of fresh root ginger, peeled and finely chopped
1 teaspoon cumin seeds, roughly crushed
2 teaspoons coriander seeds, roughly crushed
1 teaspoon black onion seeds
1 teaspoon turmeric
1 teaspoon salt
pepper

1 Preheat the slow cooker if necessary – see manufacturer's instructions. Cut a thick slice off the sides of the mango to reveal the large flat oval stone. Peel then dice all the flesh.

2 Put the mango, squash and onion in the slow cooker pot and mix in the sugar and vinegar. Add the ginger, cumin, coriander, black onion seeds and turmeric and season with salt and pepper. Cover with the lid and cook on high for 2½–2¾ hours until thick.

3 Warm 3 clean jars in the bottom of a low oven. Spoon in the chutney, place a waxed disc on top and leave to cool. Seal each jar with a screw-topped lid then label. Store in a cool place for up to 2 months. Once opened, store in the refrigerator.

Pickled plums

Pickled plums are delicious served with cold meats, salad and a jacket potato. They also make an ideal present if a few extra herbs are tied decoratively on to the clip of the jar with ribbon or raffia.

**Makes 2 x 750 ml (1¼ pint) jars
and 1 x 500 ml (17 fl oz) le parfait jar**
Preparation time: 20 minutes
Cooking time: 2–2½ hours
Cooking temperature: high
Slow cooker size: standard

750 ml (1¼ pints) white wine vinegar
500 g (1 lb) caster sugar
7 rosemary sprigs
7 thyme sprigs
7 small bay leaves
4 lavender sprigs (optional)
4 garlic cloves, unpeeled
1 teaspoon salt
½ teaspoon peppercorns
1.5 kg (3 lb) firm red plums, washed and pricked

1 Preheat the slow cooker if necessary – see manufacturer's instructions. Pour the vinegar and sugar into the cooker pot then add 4 each of the rosemary and thyme sprigs and the bay leaves, all the lavender, if using, the garlic cloves, salt and peppercorns. Cook on high for 2–2½ hours, stirring once or twice.

2 Warm the 3 clean jars in the bottom of a low oven. Pack the plums tightly into the jars. Tuck the remaining fresh herbs into the jars. Strain in the hot vinegar, making sure that the plums are completely covered, then seal tightly with rubber seals and jar lids.

3 Label the jars and leave to cool. Transfer to a cool dark cupboard and store for 3–4 weeks before using. Once opened, store in the refrigerator.

Tip
- **Add a tiny dried chilli to each jar of plums or add some broken cinnamon sticks, juniper berries and pared orange rind in place of the fresh herbs. As the plums are stored, so they will slightly lose colour.**

Tangy

A variation on lemon curd, this recipe uses lime and orange as well to create a delicious breakfast or teatime spread for toast, fruit scones or crumpets. Use three lemons instead of the citrus mix if you want to make lemon curd.

Makes 2 x 400 g (13 oz) jars
Preparation time: 25 minutes
Cooking time: 3–4 hours
Cooking temperature: low
Slow cooker size: standard

125 g (4 oz) unsalted butter
400 g (13 oz) caster sugar
grated rind and juice of 2 lemons
grated rind and juice of 1 orange
grated rind and juice of 1 lime
4 eggs, beaten

1 Preheat the slow cooker if necessary – see manufacturer's instructions. Put the butter and sugar in a saucepan, add the fruit rinds then strain in the juice. Heat gently for 2–3 minutes, stirring occasionally, until the butter has melted and the sugar dissolved.

2 Pour the mixture into a basin that will fit comfortably in your slow cooker pot. Leave to cool for 10 minutes then gradually strain in the eggs and mix well. Cover the basin with foil, put foil straps or a string pudding bowl lifter (see page 15) in the slow cooker pot and place the basin on top. Pour hot water into the cooker pot to come halfway up the sides of the basin. Add the cooker lid and cook on low for 3–4 hours until the mixture is very thick. Stir once or twice during cooking if possible.

3 Warm 2 clean jars in the bottom of a low oven. Spoon in the citrus curd, place a waxed disc on top and leave to cool. Seal each jar with a screw-top lid or a cellophane jam pot cover and an elastic band, label and store in the refrigerator. Use within 3–4 weeks.

Tip
• **A jar of home-made fruit curd makes a great present. Decorate the top of the jar by tying a circle of brown paper or double square of muslin or patterned fabric in place with raffia or ribbon. Finish by adding a new teaspoon and a gift tag.**

232

citrus curd

& apple jam

This softly set, French-style jam is made with less sugar than usual. Because timings are not so crucial in a slow cooker this recipe is a good introduction to jam making. Blackcurrants, raspberries or mulberries could be used instead of blackberries.

Makes 4 x 400 g (13 oz) jars
Preparation time: 20 minutes
Cooking time: 4–5 hours
Cooking temperature: high
Slow cooker size: standard

1 kg (2 lb) cooking apples, peeled, cored
  and chopped
500 g (1 lb) granulated sugar
grated rind of 1 lemon
2 tablespoons water or lemon juice
250 g (8 oz) blackberries

1 Preheat the slow cooker if necessary – see manufacturer's instructions. Put all the ingredients in the slow cooker pot, in the order listed opposite. Cover with the lid and cook on high for 4–5 hours, stirring once or twice during cooking. By the end of the cooking time the fruit should be thick and pulpy.

2 Warm 4 clean jars in the bottom of a low oven. Spoon in the jam, place a waxed disc on top and leave to cool. Seal each jar with a cellophane jam pot cover and an elastic band, label and store for up to 2 months in the refrigerator. The jam's low sugar content means that it does not keep as long as conventional jam and must be kept in the refrigerator.

Drinks

Hot Mexican coffee

A mix of cocoa, coffee and rum is spiked with a red chilli. Serve as it is or topped with a spoonful of lightly whipped cream and a dusting of cocoa or grated chocolate.

Serves 4

Preparation time: 10 minutes
Cooking time: 3–4 hours
Cooking temperature: low
Slow cooker size: standard

50 g (2 oz) cocoa powder
4 teaspoons instant coffee
1 litre (1¾ pints) boiling water
150 ml (¼ pint) dark rum
100 g (3½ oz) caster sugar
½ teaspoon ground cinnamon
1 large dried or fresh red chilli, halved

To decorate
150 ml (¼) pint double cream
2 tablespoons grated dark chocolate,
4 small dried chillies (optional)

1 Preheat the slow cooker if necessary – see manufacturer's instructions. Put the cocoa and instant coffee in a bowl and mix to a smooth paste with a little of the boiling water.

2 Pour the cocoa paste into the slow cooker pot, add the remaining boiling water, the rum, sugar, cinnamon and red chilli and mix together.

3 Cover and cook the toddy on low for 3–4 hours until piping hot or until required. Stir well, then ladle it into heatproof glasses. Whip the cream until it is just beginning to hold its shape and spoon a little into each glass. Decorate each drink with a little grated chocolate and a dried chilli, if using.

Tip
• **Use level teaspoons of coffee or the flavour will be too overpowering.**

Honeyed cider
& spiced apple

Put this on to cook while you find your boots and coats, then lower the temperature just as you go out for a weekend walk. It's a welcome treat to come back to and a change from the heavier, red-wine based versions of hot toddies.

Serves 6

Preparation time: 10 minutes
Cooking time: 4–5 hours
Cooking temperature: high and low
Slow cooker size: standard

2 dessert apples
12 cloves
2 cinnamon sticks
75 g (3 oz) set honey
1 litre (1¾ pints) vintage dry cider

1 Preheat the slow cooker if necessary – see manufacturer's instructions. Core each apple and cut it into thick slices. Press the cloves into 12 apple slices and put them in the slow cooker pot.

2 Break the cinnamon sticks in half and add them to the apples with the honey and cider.

3 Cover and cook on high for 1 hour, then reduce the temperature to low for 3–4 hours or until piping hot. You can cook this toddy for longer if liked. Stir well and ladle into heatproof glasses to serve.

Tip
• **If you have some calvados (apple brandy), you might like to add a little to the toddy just before serving.**

Hot citrus burst

Serves 6

Preparation time: 10 minutes
Cooking time: 4–5 hours
Cooking temperature: high and low
Slow cooker size: standard

8 cardamom pods
rind of 1 lemon and juice of 3 lemons
rind of 1 orange and juice of 3 oranges
125 g (4 oz) set honey
100 g (3½ oz) caster sugar
750 ml (1¼ pints) cold water
150 ml (¼ pint) whisky

1 Preheat the slow cooker if necessary – see manufacturer's instructions. Crush the cardamom pods using a pestle and mortar or with the end of a rolling pin and put the pods and seeds into the slow cooker pot.

2 Add the fruit rinds and juice, honey, sugar, water and whisky. Cover and cook on high for 1 hour, then reduce the temperature to low for 3–4 hours, until piping hot, or longer if liked. Stir well and ladle into small, heatproof glasses.

Apricot & brandy ratafia

Serves 6

Preparation time: 15 minutes
Cooking time: 3–4 hours
Cooking temperature: low
Slow cooker size: standard

1 teaspoon sunflower oil
40 g (1½ oz) flaked almonds
100 g (3½ oz) ready-to-eat dried apricots
1 litre (1¾ pints) white grape juice
150 ml (¼ pint) brandy
75 g (3 oz) caster sugar

1 Preheat the slow cooker if necessary – see manufacturer's instructions. Heat the oil in a frying pan, add the almonds and cook, stirring, until golden all over.

2 Add the almonds and apricots to the slow cooker and pour in the grape juice and brandy. Add the sugar, cover and cook on low for 3–4 hours until piping hot or until required. Stir well and ladle into heatproof glasses to serve.

Hot Jamaican punch

Serves 6

Preparation time: 10 minutes
Cooking time: 3–4 hours
Cooking temperature: high and low
Slow cooker size: standard

juice of 3 limes
300 ml (½ pint) dark rum
300 ml (½ pint) ginger wine
600 ml (1 pint) cold water
75 g (3 oz) caster sugar

To decorate

1 lime, thinly sliced
2 slices of pineapple, cored but skin left on and
    cut into pieces

1 Preheat the slow cooker if necessary – see manufacturer's instructions. Strain the lime juice into the slow cooker pot and discard the pips. Add the rum, ginger wine, water and sugar, cover and cook on high for 1 hour.

2 Reduce the heat to low and cook for 2–3 hours until the punch is piping hot or until you are ready to serve. Stir well, then ladle into heatproof glasses and add a slice of lime and 2 pieces of pineapple to each glass.

Grossmutter's punch

Serves 8

Preparation time: 5 minutes
Cooking time: 3–4 hours
Cooking temperature: high and low
Slow cooker size: standard

750 ml (1¼ pints) red wine (75 cl bottle)
600 ml (1 pint) cold water
150 ml (¼ pint) dark rum
1 'breakfast tea' teabag
125 g (4 oz) caster sugar
6 cinnamon sticks, to serve

1 Preheat the slow cooker if necessary – see manufacturer's instructions. Pour the wine, measured water and rum into the slow cooker pot. Add the teabag and sugar, cover and cook on high for 1 hour.

2 Stir the punch and remove the teabag. Reduce the heat to low and cook for 2–3 hours until it is piping hot or until required.

3 Stir just before serving, ladle the punch into heatproof glasses and serve with a cinnamon stick stirrer in each glass.

Lemon cordial

Keep this cordial in the door of the refrigerator then dilute as required with cold water or sparkling mineral water and lots of ice. Wonderfully refreshing, it is free from unnecessary additives. Tartaric acid is available from pharmacies.

Makes about 20 glasses

Preparation time: 10 minutes
Cooking time: 3–4 hours
Cooking temperatures: high and low
Slow cooker size: standard

3 lemons, washed and thinly sliced
625 g (1 1/4 lb) granulated sugar
900 ml (1 1/2 pints) boiling water
25 g (1 oz) tartaric acid
mint or lemon balm, to decorate (optional)

1 Preheat the slow cooker if necessary – see manufacturer's instructions. Add the lemon slices to the slow cooker pot with the sugar and boiling water, stir well until the sugar is almost all dissolved then cover with the lid and cook on high for 1 hour.

2 Reduce the heat and cook on low for 2–3 hours until the lemons are almost translucent. Switch off the slow cooker and stir in the tartaric acid. Leave to cool.

3 Remove and discard some of the sliced lemons using a slotted spoon. Transfer the cordial and remaining lemons to 2 sterilized screw-topped wide-necked bottles or storage jars. Seal well, label and store in the refrigerator for up to 1 month.

4 To serve, dilute the cordial with water in a ratio of 1:3, adding a few of the sliced lemons for decoration, ice cubes and sprigs of fresh mint or lemon balm if available.

Spiced citrus cup

Warming and refreshing, this non-alcoholic punch is perfect for any guests who have to drive home. Vary the combination of fruit teas and spices to suit your taste. Try mixing cranberry, elderflower and raspberry tea with cranberry juice or perhaps camomile and elderflower tea with crushed coriander seeds and orange juice.

Makes 8–10 glasses

Preparation time: 10 minutes
Cooking time: 2–3 hours
Cooking temperature: low
Slow cooker size: standard

6 lemon and ginger or lemon and camomile herbal
   infusion tea bags
1.5 litres (2½ pints) boiling water
150 g (5 oz) caster sugar
3 tablespoons thick set honey
300 ml (½ pint) orange juice (from a carton)
2 cinnamon sticks, halved
10 cardamom pods, crushed
1 orange, sliced

1 Preheat the slow cooker if necessary – see manufacturer's instructions. Put the tea bags in the slow cooker pot. Pour in the boiling water then add the sugar, honey, orange juice, cinnamon, cardamom pods and their black seeds and sliced orange. Mix the ingredients together.

2 Cover with the lid and cook on low for 2–3 hours. Strain, if liked, to remove the tea bags and spices then ladle into glasses.

Mulled cranberry & red wine

Makes 8–10 glasses

Preparation time: 10 minutes
Cooking time: 4–5 hours
Cooking temperature: high and low
Slow cooker size: standard

750 ml (1¼ pints) inexpensive red wine (75 cl bottle)
600 ml (1 pint) cranberry juice (from a carton)
100 ml (3½ fl oz) brandy, rum, vodka or orange
   liqueur
100 g (3½ oz) caster sugar
1 orange
8 cloves
1–2 cinnamon sticks, depending on size

To serve
8–10 long rosemary sprigs
1 orange
1 lime
2–3 bay leaves
few fresh cranberries

1 Preheat the slow cooker if necessary – see manufacturer's instructions. Pour the red wine, cranberry juice and brandy or other alcohol into the slow cooker pot then stir in the sugar.

2 Cut the orange into 8 segments and stud each piece with a clove. Break the cinnamon sticks into large pieces and add to the pot with the orange pieces. Cover with the lid and cook on high for 1 hour. Reduce the temperature and cook on low for 3–4 hours.

3 To serve, place a sprig of rosemary in each heatproof glass. Replace the orange with new pieces and add the bay leaves and cranberries. Ladle into glasses, keeping back the fruit and herbs if liked.

Tip
• **Replace the cranberry juice with 300 ml (½ pint) orange juice (from a carton) and 300 ml (½ pint) water if preferred.**

Index

Acknowledgements

The author and publisher would like to thank Morphy
Richards for loaning a range of different sized slow
cookers for the testing and photography of this book.
For further information, visit the Morphy Richards
website on www.morphyrichards.co.uk or write to
Morphy Richards, Talbot Road, Mexborough, South
Yorkshire, S64 8AJ. They would also like to thank
Prima for supplying a range of slow cookers for
photography. For further information, write to
Nu-World UK Ltd, Prima, 15 (2D) Springfield
Commercial Centre, Bagley Lane, Pudsey, LS28 5LY.

Executive Editor: Nicola Hill
Managing Editor: Clare Churly
Editor: Amy Corbett
Executive Art Editor: Leigh Jones
Designers: Keith Williams, Miranda Harvey
Photographer: Stephen Conroy
Home Economist: Sara Lewis
Stylists: Claire Hunt, Rachel Jukes
Senior Production Controller: Manjit Sihra

Special photography:
© Octopus Publishing Group Limited/Stephen Conroy